The Day-Care Dilemma

Women and Children First

Marian Blum
Wellesley College

LexingtonBooks
D.C. Heath and Company
Lexington, Massachusetts
Toronto

Library of Congress Cataloging in Publication Data

Blum, Marian.
The day-care dilemma.

Includes bibliographical references and index.
1. Day care centers—United States. I. Title.
HV854.B57 1983 362.7′12′0973 82-47777
ISBN 0-669-05604-9

Published simultaneously in Canada

Printed in the United States of America

International Standard Book Number: 0-669-05604-9

Library of Congress Catalog Card Number: 82-47777

To Leon

Contents

Figures and Tables

Figures

Tables

Preface and Acknowledgments

This book is the result of two decades of professional work with young children, their parents, and their teachers. My purpose is to be an advocate for children, not an adversary to any group or institution. I use feminine pronouns in most of the book not because I am unconcerned about the lives of men and boys but because I wish to emphasize my concerns about the lives and rights of women. All of the anecdotes and case histories are fictional composites of actual experiences, and any resemblances to real children and adults are coincidental.

I am grateful to many people at Wellesley College for their interest, encouragement, and assistance; but the following deserve special mention: the Psychology Department faculty, especially Blythe Clinchy; also David Pillemer, Sheila Brachfeld-Child, and Elissa Koff; the staff of the Child Study Center, including Lynn Burke, Ann Schwarz, Mary Ucci, and especially Terry Rourke; Irene Laursen and other librarians at the Margaret Clapp and Science Center libraries; and Fran Sessa, class of 1985. I appreciate the support I received from Wellesley College by means of the Mary Baldwin Weston Fund.

Many friends, colleagues, and relatives helped in small and large ways. I thank them all. But, in particular, I thank: Barbara Pastan and Robert Mezer, M.D., especially for their help on medical issues; my colleagues and friends Muriel Hirt, Marilyn Keilson, and Martha McGandy for general assistance and encouragement; Florence Marcus, Harry Mezer, Ben Selling, and Margaret Zusky for initial input and prodding about writing; my sister and colleague, Lois Mezer, and my mother, Rose Sternlieb, for many years of advice and encouragement.

My daughter, Amy, her husband, Doug Bergner, my son, Jim, and my husband, Leon, know what important contributions they have made. I thank them for their patience, their devotion, and much more.

1 Introduction

There are long traditions of women and children being first. In fiction and in fact, particularly in times of disaster—since it was first issued as a naval order during the sinking of the *Birkenhead* in 1852—the maxim has been "women and children first." But it is an empty maxim, for women do not come first, especially when the economic realities of their lives are examined. Although it has been found that most young women expect to marry and be supported by a husband, the realities are that the majority of women work and most women work out of economic necessity. Only a tiny fraction of those families headed by women are above the poverty level. Yet, most women continue to choose or accept traditionally female occupations because those occupations are all that are available and because they offer flexibility and easy ways to enter and exit the labor force. The price women pay for this work pattern is that they lose out on higher paying career opportunities, promotions, and pensions.[1]

Young mothers pay an even higher price. The conflicts between work and childrearing become, most often, no-win situations. Like their mothers of the 1950s, when it comes to working versus staying home, they are damned if they do and damned if they don't. Women of the fifties were caught smack in the middle of a great social and political upheaval; they had grown up expecting one set of values or common goals, and were told, in the middle of it all, that those values and goals were all wrong. If life was good, then the woman was a parasite. If life was desperate, it was because of a male, chauvinistic society. Those mothers of the 1950s who went to work early were made to feel guilty and negligent. Those who stayed home were made to feel guilty and lazy. The same thing seems to be happening to women in the eighties. They are not getting necessary advice, support, or help from either their peers or their predecessors. Denied constitutional guarantees of equality of social, legal, and economic rights, women are more *last* than *first*.

Children fare even less well. Children, too, do not have specific constitutional rights: they are, essentially, the property of their parents. According to current statistics, there are over one-million reported cases of child abuse per year in the United States.[2] Children are exploited by corporations ranging from television networks to blue-jean manufacturers.[3] They are victimized by drug dealers and pornographers and many are lured into early experimentation with alcohol and sex. Of more relevance to the subject of day care, however, is the fact that there are approximately one-million licensed day-care-center slots for the estimated 8-million preschoolers whose mothers work.[4] Approximately 3.5 million are cared for by relatives and another 3.5 million in family-day-care homes.[5] There are an estimated 20-thousand preschool children who are left alone, to care for themselves, while their parents work.[6] Many people see the expansion of day-care centers as the solution to the problems of both women and children.

Day care has become as American as apple pie and baseball. Everyone, with few exceptions,[7] says that day care is here to stay. Some of the discussions are reminiscent of the plans for evacuation in the event of a nuclear attack. Whether for it or against it, whether one thinks it is healthy or not, everyone sees it as a given, as a demographic necessity. "It has become a necessary service to many parents."[8] "Good child care is crucial to women's liberation."[9] "Day care is an idea whose time has come."[10] "Coming out against (day-care centers) now would be like coming out against the automobile."[11] "Child care is now and will continue to be a necessity for America's economy, its families, and its children."[12] "Day care is a fact of modern life, no longer a debatable issue."[13] Day care is like a roller coaster that cannot be stopped.

The popularity of day care as a subject can be seen in the numerous books, magazine articles, and newspaper reports about it. Radio and television editorials endorse it. Cartoonists deal with it. Day care has been studied by various women's groups including the National Council of Jewish Women, the League of Women Voters, and the Junior League. It has been researched by psychologists and sociologists, by educators and economists.

If day care is a popular topic, it is also an emotional one that tends to polarize people. Its advocates see it as essential for women if they are to fulfill themselves psychologically and if they are to achieve their rightful place in the working world. They see day care as a positive experience for children, for their physical, social, emotional, and cognitive development. Some of its critics, however, see it as the abandonment of children by the narcissistic "me" generation, an abdication of the parental role. They see it as undermining the family in the United States, as a socialistic way to raise children. Other critics, however, view it as an extension and exacerbation of the "corporate paradigm."[14] Still others, who see the ambiguities—the advantages as well as the drawbacks—whose opinions fall somewhere between the two poles, are scorned, often with shrillness and stridency, by both sides. Day care is, of course, an economic and political issue. Some maintain that without it, young families cannot survive. They need two incomes to manage in these inflationary times. Others see the fact that more women are working as a contribution to the very inflation that makes survival so difficult. Still others lament the economic situation of day-care providers whose low salary is matched by a publicly perceived low status.

Politicians and policymakers must respond to the day-care issue. They must base decisions on their constituencies' pressures and needs and, to some extent, on the available research. Finally, through compromise and negotiation, they must determine priorities for spending. The bottom line in their eyes, however, is not whether day care is best for children or for women but how much money day care will either save or cost.

Above all, day care is an issue about children and about women. Children in day care have been observed, compared, tested, scrutinized, and measured. Unfortunately, they are too young to have been interviewed about their experiences. Women who work in day care and women who utilize day care have been studied also, but to a lesser extent than the children. Their position has not yet received the kind of attention it merits.

Day care is full of complexities, ambiguities, and ironies caused by the very nature of the institution: it must serve the needs of young children, their parents, their caregivers, and society at large, all at the same time. This role would not be so unusual except that the needs and goals of each of these constituencies are often in conflict. Trade-offs to resolve those conflicts are usually at the expense of one or more of the other constituencies. For instance, if the federal government subsidizes a day-care center for children of migrant farm workers, is its main constituency the children, the parents, the landowners, or, in a macroeconomic sense, the entire country?

A center that considers its major constituency children would have a larger than most commonly recommended or required staff-to-child ratio (that is, more staff to fewer children). It would have spacious, sunny facilities; good, well-maintained indoor and outdoor equipment; plentiful supplies; nutritious and attractive food; adequate funds for janitorial services and sanitation; and comprehensive health services. It would have several well-paid caregivers or teachers with each small group of children, so that there would always be adequate care and so that the teachers could take needed sick leaves, vacations, and mental-health days without damaging the functioning of the class or the sense of security of any individual child. There would be separate areas for play, for eating, for sleeping, and for isolation during last-minute minor illnesses. Because the staff would be well paid, and because the work load would be lighter, there would be less turnover, so that a young child entering at age two could predictably have the same teachers at ages three and four. There would be enough funds to provide for frequent staff meetings and workshops, for courses, and for other in-service staff training. There would be adequate funds for consultation with social workers, clinical psychologists, and nutritionists and for the implementation of a supportive parent program. The center would be very expensive.

None of the above would ever be possible in a center that saw as its prime constituency the parents, for that would necessitate more realistic budgeting, which, in turn, would mean cutting back on expensive items such as staff, space, consultations, fringe benefits, and other presumed luxuries. In its obligations to serve parents, the center could not be as child-centered as the previous utopian example.

This book explores some of the paradoxes of day care. It attempts to point out the realities of contemporary day care, to show what the quality of life is like in some high-quality day-care centers of the early 1980s. It will show the daily experience and routine for children and for their adult caretakers, the large majority of whom are, of course, women. It will show that the day-care-center system is one that, in many cases, contributes more to placing women and children last rather than first.

This book will concentrate on children of middle-class professional parents in all-day rather than half-day programs. Nursery schools or other programs that last for just a few hours daily are quite different from all-day day-care centers. Unfortunately, many authorities confuse, and even combine, the two. Yet the families who use nursery schools have a different orientation from day-care families—and the shorter hours and differing needs present other kinds of stresses on children, parents, staff, and even on space.

The issues of the children of poverty, both inner city and rural, although essentially the same—after all, all children need safe, nurturing, stimulating, competent care—offer enough differences so that other kinds of discussions might be more appropriate. But certainly, some of the warnings, concerns, and ultimate resolutions can be generalized to apply to all women and children.

This book does not deal with the school-aged child. There is a current proliferation of after-school programs for elementary-school-aged children. Instead of being the old so-called latchkey children, they are the stay-all-day-in-school children. To some observers, both day care for children of the poor and in-school after-school care are additional examples of women and children being put not first but last.

This book will not deal with child care in other countries. China, the Soviet Union, Israel, and the Scandinavian countries are cited frequently as societies that cherish their young and, simultaneously, value their women. It has been said that "child care in this country is put to shame by the comprehensive systems in many other nations."[15] There are enough philosophical, political, economic, and social differences to make most comparisons impractical. In addition, there would have to be a reliance on secondary sources—and there is some evidence that much of what has been written has been based on brief, often superficial, visits to model facilities rather than on thorough explorations of the actual day-care experience.

Nor is this a how-to-do-it book, with five easy answers. The book will, in fact, ask questions rather than answer them. It will pose many problems, many dilemmas. The answers, ultimately, will have to come from concerned, informed parents and professionals who must seek new and creative solutions to these serious, sometimes overwhelming, questions.

2 Children as Things

The women's movement of the 1960s and the 1970s rightly called national attention to the inequities and injustices facing women. At home and in the marketplace, women were, and essentially still are, second-class citizens. Women were unable to pass the equal-rights amendment (ERA) despite a congressional extension and despite the fact that thirty-five of the required thirty-eight state legislatures needed for ratification had voted for it. The states had not rejected a proposed constitutional change since 1924, when they rejected a child-labor amendment. The rejection of ERA is another case of women and children not being first. The proposed amendment states: "Equality of rights under the law shall not be denied or abridged on account of sex." Polls showed that over half of those who had heard of ERA were in favor of it.[1] It did not give women precedence, firstness, in any setting. Despite its opponents warnings, it would not have created havoc in lavatories; nor would it have impaired our national defense.

Women are even more last than first when the economics of their lives are examined. In 1981, 51 percent of U.S. women aged sixteen and over were working.[2] Of the thirty-eight-million women in the labor force, twenty-six million, or seven out of ten, work out of economic necessity.[3] When age is added to gender, the economic situation is even worse: the fastest growing poverty group in the United States is made up of single women over the age of fifty.

Motherhood complicates the issue even more. There are almost seventeen-million working mothers with children under eighteen.[4] Demographers predict that by 1990 only 25 percent of married women will be full-time housewives and mothers.[5] Women still have the major responsibility for child care. Although there are isolated stories of role reversals and fifty-fifty sharing, the large majority of working women continue to bear the simultaneous burden of running a household and raising children.

An article in the *New York Times*, "Balancing Children and a Legal Career," describes a program called "You, Your Child, Your Career," Designed for women attorneys, the program deals with the difficulties an associate must overcome to achieve a partnership without overly long hours and night and weekend work. Clearly the women interviewed had made career sacrifices to have children and to have some share in their care. Nowhere in the article of approximately fifteen-hundred words is mention made of husbands or fathers making similar sacrifices.[6]

Statistics bear this out. In 1965, men averaged nine hours a week in household chores and child care; in 1975, they averaged 9.7 hours. Women, on the other hand, spent 28.8 hours in such work in 1965; in 1975 they had reduced that figure to 24.9 hours.[7] Yet, since 1970 the greatest labor-force increases have occurred among married women under age thirty-five with children under three.

As Pamela Daniels and Kathy Weingarten point out in *Sooner or Later: The Timing of Parenthood in Adult Lives*, "regardless of generation or politics, level of education or career ambition, regardless of whether parenthood comes 'early' or 'late' or 'very late,' women have been and still are the primary caretakers of children in our society."[8] The women's movement, then, although it has made many gains for the status of women, still has much to accomplish. And, despite its positive gains, the movement has also had some negative consequences.

Many women with high corporate ambitions are delaying childbirth until they are well established in the business world. If a competent woman must concentrate on her career to solidify her position in a company (or a hospital or a university), she often must wait until her late thirties or early forties to take time off to have children. According to the National Center for Health Statistics, the number of first births to women over thirty more than doubled in the decade from 1970 to 1980.[9] Yet medical authorities advise that the ages of twenty-five to twenty-nine are the ideal times to have a first child. This discrepancy raises some difficult personal and social issues.

The first problem older couples face is the risk of infertility. "Human reproductive capacity peaks for both sexes in the mid 20s, and thereafter appears to decline—rapidly so among women over 30 and men over 40."[10] In *You're Not Too Old to Have a Baby*, Jane Price discusses "the psychological problems that set in when a couple finds they can't have the child they have longed for—feelings of grief, inadequacy, mutual suspicion, embarrassment, even damaged sexual performance. Fertility experts have found older couples especially frustrated by repeated failures at conception, pressured by the realization that their time is about to run out. Such problems can't be glossed over lightly."[11]

Once couples have overcome the risks of infertility due to age, they must cope with the risks of early miscarriages. Daniels and Weingarten cite a study that found that the miscarriage rates for first pregnancies increased significantly with age. For women in their twenties, the rate for miscarriages was 40 per 1000; for women thirty to thirty-four, the rate was 75 per 1000; and for women over age thirty-five, the rate was 150 per 1000.[12]

Still another problem for older couples is the greater risk of having a handicapped child. Although there is increasing research into paternal age as a cause of some chromosomal abnormalities,[13] the relationship of the mother's age and Down's Syndrome births cannot be overlooked. According to one publication by the U.S. Department of Health and Human Services, women under age thirty have a 1 in 1000 chance of having a child with Down's Syndrome. At age thirty-five, the chance is 1 in 400; at age forty it is 1 in 105. At age forty-eight it is 1 in 12.[14]

Recent research by Richard L. Naeye for the Collaborative Perinatal Project of the National Institute of Neurological and Communicative Disorders and Stroke has raised some other questions about the age of the mother. Naeye's work has dealt with the blood flow to the fetus. He has concluded that in the normal aging process, the blood vessels, including uterine blood vessels, become stiff and do not expand enough during pregnancy to adequately supply the growing fetus. In an examination of the data from over forty-four-thousand pregnancies, Naeye found that there was a death rate just before or just after birth of 25 per 1000 babies for mothers seventeen to nineteen years old. That rate increased to 69 per 1000 for mothers over thirty-nine. Naeye believes that 50 percent of these deaths involved impaired blood flow to the uterus.[15]

Of course, medical science continues to make major and somewhat reassuring advances in obstetrics and genetics. In one study by the Birth Defects Branch of the Center for Disease Control in Atlanta, it was shown "that after eliminating those birth defects that could be prevented or eliminated by detection techniques . . . for mothers from 35 to 44 years of age, the risk of bearing an infant with a severe birth defect was reduced to a level comparable to that for younger women. The 30-35-year-old age group appears to have very little greater risk than their 20-year-old counterparts if *mothers have good prenatal medical care and fetal detection* (italic in original)."[16]

Knowledge of the risks of late childbearing and the use of prenatal detection measures such as amniocentesis do ease some concerns, but they also create an additional burden. As Daniels and Weingarten point out, they affect "couples' psychological experience of pregnancy and childbearing, intensifying feelings of vulnerability in an already vulnerable time, and clouding for a while the anticipation of parenthood."[17]

Despite medical progress, the data on older women and childbearing and the psychological ramifications of that data begin to make some of the victories of the women's movement seem pyrrhic; they seem to be victories achieved at significant human cost.

Another result of the women's movement has been its emphasis on materialism. It criticized men for making women into possessions and love objects. It criticized women for allowing this to happen. Then the movement sent an apparently contradictory message: the only real value a person could have was through paid employment. Everything had to have a monetary reward to be meaningful. Thus, women who had worked as volunteers on hospital committees or had managed political campaigns were made to feel that they were exploited by a dominant male society. Women who had gained satisfactions from homemaking and child care were belittled even more. Ironically, many feminists were critical of men for being materialistic—but then saw material success as the solution to the problems of women.

The women's movement had an interesting effect on the education of young children. Feminists influenced teachers to purge nursery schools and day-care centers of classic children's books because they had pictures of women wearing aprons or baking cakes.[18] What used to be called the doll corner became the house corner, or better still, the sociodramatic play area. Community helpers were renamed firefighters, letter carriers, and policepersons. References to doctors were preferable in the feminine gender, while references to nurses were sometimes masculine. In overcoming all of the old sex-role stereotypes, the emphasis was always on each child achieving his or her potential. Yet, while a girl could hope to be an astronaut or a president, rarely could she aspire to be a housewife. Even those little girls who chose ballerina as a future occupation were sometimes looked upon as relics of the old chauvinist days! Being an acrobat was more desirable because that did not require the fluffy, stereotypically feminine tutu.

The message sent to young children was certainly one of hope and optimism. For both boys and girls it was a message that children could grow freely and achieve whatever they were best at or whatever they liked the most. But, underlying it all was a message of material success, a message of salaried employment being the ultimate goal. This emphasis on materialism means that just as one can achieve anything, one can also buy anything. One can purchase convenience foods, one can purchase bigger and better appliances. And one can purchase child care. This emphasis on materialism has also transformed children into products, things, objects. They must produce; they must perform; they must prove their worth. Stress on production and performance has meant hurrying the child chronologically.[19] Children are expected to accomplish adult tasks earlier and earlier. Parents will deliver a two-year-old child to a day-care center and respond to tears with a pat on the back and the words, "Oh, Nancy, stop acting like a baby."

Another example of this pressure to achieve or behave beyond their normal competencies is seen in children's art work. Art education in preschools and day-care centers has always stressed process over product: the actual experience of working in clay or with paints is more meaningful for the young child than the finished product. Besides, children develop abilities in art in a developmental, sequential pattern, gradually moving from scribbling to representational art. But parents who see their children more as possessions, who want to bask in the reflected glory of early achievements, who do not value childhood as an important time of life, tend to push the child into doing more representational, copying, "adultlike" art. With stresses on monetary and personal success so strong, parents forget that childhood is part of life, not just preparation for life—and many parents expect the day-care center to share the burden of speeding up the development of the child.

This pervasive materialism has also raised everyone's economic expectations. The more that paid work is valued, the more it is sought; and as more money is earned, more material possessions become desired. It is a self-perpetuating spiral and children are part of, perhaps even victims of, that spiral. They are seen as desirable possessions rather than as living, feeling, growing organisms with particular, individualized needs. In our materialistic society, we have dehumanized our children and have made them things.

Newspaper articles offer examples of this dehumanization of children. One woman, enrolled in an infant-care course, is noted as showing surprise when she learned that parents should be talking and singing to babies as they bathe them.[20] Another mother describes her day at the office with her three-week-old baby and says that she is able to type while she's nursing; she is able to talk on the telephone while she's nursing; she is even able to close important business deals while she is nursing![21]

It is another irony of the day-care issue that when women, who had been treated like things, like objects, like possessions, finally attempted to achieve some status of their own, they turned to the next most vulnerable group, children, and began to treat them like things, objects, possessions. It is as if women, in order to scramble up the ladder of the man's world, have had to adopt some of the very characteristics of men that were attacked initially.

Some specialists in eating disorders of young women have suggested that one cause for the rampant spread of the disease bulimia might be a partial consequence of the promises of the women's movement. Bulimics gorge themselves on huge amounts of food and then vomit. It is perhaps a response to one of the messages of the women's movement: you can have it all, but you don't have to suffer any adverse consequences. Eat whatever you'd like, and as much as you'd like, but still stay thin just by regurgitating what you have consumed.[22] Some parental attitudes toward children seem to echo this syndrome. Young parents are told that they can have it all. They can have stimulating professional careers, high-powered work, active social lives, and young children. But, in some ways some parents are ridding themselves of their children just as bulimics are regurgitating their food. Many are not accepting the responsiblities, or the consequences, of having children. They do not want to raise them, they do not want to nurture them as long as they can hire others, at not too high a price, to do so. Some even seek twenty-four-hour day care and fifty-two weeks a year of school.

Of course, many forces in our society, not just the women's movement, are responsible for the dehumanization of our children. School officials in West Virginia took a five-year-old child to court for being disruptive in his kindergarten class.[23] The Federal Bureau of Investigation has distributed posters with the pictures of fugitives and their children to pediatricians and family physicians. The mailings include information about the children's medical histories so that doctors can be on the alert to find these families. Children are being used to entrap their parents; their innocence is ignored.[24]

Perhaps the most poignant example of dehumanization is the issue of unwanted lives. There are growing numbers of lawsuits that claim that medical negligence led to *wrongful life* and *wrongful birth*. Parents of defective children, and handicapped children themselves, are the plaintiffs in the wrongful-life suits. In wrongful-birth suits, parents of healthy but unplanned children are suing for the costs of raising those wrongful children. They sue for damages, claiming that the births were due to failed tubal ligations, failed vasectomies, or failed abortions. Courts have varied in their decisions, but a 1981 Illinois decision awarded parents the costs of rearing and educating an unplanned child. Its ruling was that a couple's right to limit procreation did not lessen the uniqueness of life.[25]

This pattern of litigation raises some very complex issues for physicians, for right-to-lifers, for abortion advocates, and for the legal profession. It is also an important issue for anyone concerned with the lives of children. For, if children are things, if children are possessions, then people do not want damaged goods. Nor do people want the unexpected. They are unwilling to take responsibility for their own actions and for their own offspring. They are unwilling to accept something as old-fashioned as an accident of nature or of chance. Someone outside must be accountable. If a handicapped child is born, sue the doctor.

Unfortunately, in another one of those paradoxes about day-care centers, this trend toward dehumanization is happening in the very institutions that should be the most caring,the most nurturant, the most humanitarian; it is happening in day-care centers and in other services for children. Human babies are born not in litters but, usually, one at a time. If, however, they are to be raised in large groups, with multiple caretakers and with several babies to each adult, then methods have to be devised to make that care possible. One day-care center uses color-coded baby bottles to avoid mix-ups of formula.[26] One must wonder whether babies so fed see bottles of ketchup or Riesling wine and begin to crave their milk.

Another infant center had an interested, involved parent group that worked with the staff to create an eating facility that would be more efficient for the limited number of staff available. They designed and built a narrow drop-leaf table that was suspended against a wall when not in use. At mealtime, the leaf was lowered and there were four slots in it to place the babies in their infant seats. One teacher sat opposite and fed all four at once. Each baby could see the one next to her, but they were essentially all in a row, as if on an assembly line. The amount of eye contact the teacher could make with each baby was of course limited. She could not carry on continued chitchats with the babies because another one was always waiting for a spoonful of lunch.

Day-care centers also have to devise ways to take children on walks, excursions, and field trips. These worthwhile outings serve many developmental purposes: they provide fresh air and a change of scenery from the regular classroom; they broaden the horizons of the children by enabling them to see nature or stores or construction. A short walk with a child can reveal details about leaves or manhole covers or traffic lights or dogs that the average adult would never notice.

Walks for day-care children are somewhat different. To keep children safe, caretakers have had to improvise various methods. One popular solution is borrowed from the world of pets: harnesses and leashes. (See figure 2-1.) With this system, one caretaker can take six children for a walk. But a careful look at one caretaker with six children raises some questions. Can one caretaker respond to the questions, share the immediate glee or fear, attempt to satisfy the sense of wonder of six small children? How would the teacher cope with a fall, a badly scraped knee? Would she hook the other five leashes to a handy hydrant while she tended to the injured child? Or

Source: Courtesy of Wide World Photos.

Figure 2-1. Harnesses and Leashes

would all the children have to return to the day-care center for the treatment of one child? What happens if one child spots an interesting rock and wants to stop to pick it up? Is it possible to allow her to do so while the other five are still walking? If one child starts to fall, is there a domino effect?

Some teachers who do not like the idea of harnesses and leashes for young children and who have more lavish budgets use, instead, carts for their field trips. (See figure 2-2.) The cart is less risky than leashes in terms of falls. But if a child spots something interesting and wants to stop and explore it, it is impossible. In addition, her vision of the outside world is limited by her position on the cart; that is, if she is facing east and hears an interesting sound to the west, she cannot look to satisfy her curiosity.

If there is something dehumanizing about the use of leashes and carts for transporting children, there are even more dehumanizing characteristics

Source: Courtesy of Community Playthings, Rifton, N.Y.

Figure 2-2. Wagon for Six

in the cribs designed and manufactured for group care. Most standard cribs are fifty-four-inches long, thirty-inches wide and about forty-four-inches high. The average two-year old is thirty-four-inches tall, so this size crib gives her room to move around, to stretch, to kick. Standard cribs, however, take up a great deal of space, and space is a major expense for day-care centers. So, there are specially designed cribs for group care that make more efficient use of space and personnel.

Some cribs designed for institutional use have clear acrylic end panels that allow caretakers to see a child from various angles and distances in the room. These cribs are forty-inches long, twenty-five-inches wide, and of the same height as most standard cribs.[27] Other cribs are described by their manufacturers as "large enough for the child yet small enough to have six or eight cribs in a room."[28] These cribs are thirty-nine-inches long, twenty-six-inches wide, and thirty-six-inches high. (See figure 2-3).

But the most efficient cribs for institutional use are the double-decker ones. They consist of four units, two up and two down, with closed sides. (See figure 2-4.) Thc crib slats are set into sliding doors that lock into place for safety. "The sitter can keep four babies happy and in open view comfortably without constant individual attention,"[29] says one manufacturer. "Gates lock closed and child can sleep or play with [sic] constant individual attention,"[30] says another.

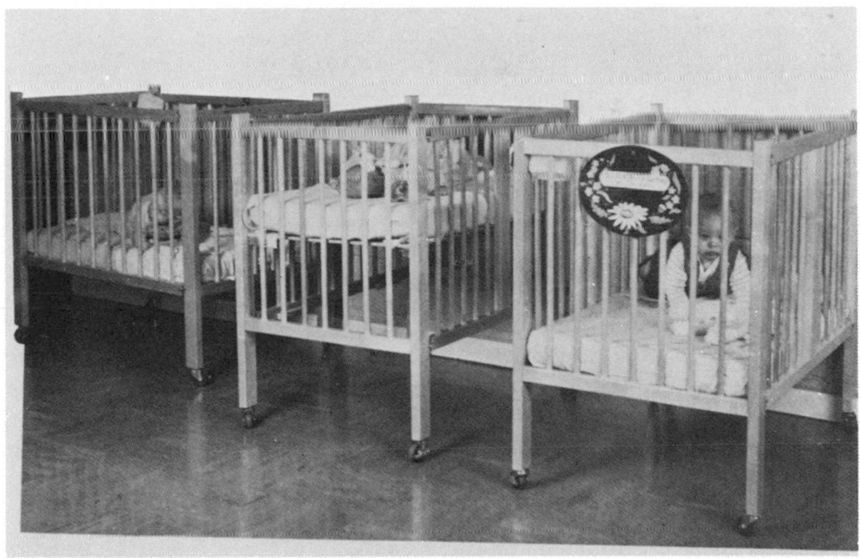

Source: Courtesy of Community Playthings, Rifton, N.Y.

Figure 2-3. Small Cribs

Source: Courtesy of Hertz Furniture Systems Co., New York.

Figure 2-4. Nursery Cribs

It is important to look carefully at these institutional cribs, especially the double-decker ones. It is important, too, to compare them to standard cribs. Each unit is thirty-seven-inches long, twenty-eight-inches wide, and thirty-four-inches high; it is, then, sixteen inches shorter and ten inches lower than a standard crib. How is the thirty-four-inch-tall two-year-old child going to stand up in the lower-level thirty-four-inch-high crib? Where does the staff put mobiles for the infant to grasp, chatter at, or play with? Each infant can see out of one side only because she faces wood with "non-toxic brown-white speckle-tone enamel" on three sides and above her head. What happens when she hears sounds from the other cribs but cannot see into them? How can she learn about the world around her? When the caregiver approaches the four-child unit, does the child feel attended to because she thinks the caregiver is coming to her? Does she stretch out her arms only to see the teacher direct her attention to an unseen child in a neighboring berth?

For crib babies who need some rocking, technology has produced a battery-operated crib-sized hammock. Of course, its cost of $39.95 might make it expensive for most day-care centers.[31] Perhaps it will serve as a prototype for less expensive, institutional models.

For the child who is too old or too large for a crib, there are several types of cots. (See figures 2-5 and 2-6.) Some are made of aluminum frames that are about a foot off the floor and have a resting surface of stretched canvas or other fabric. But there are also molded plastic cots that sit right on the floor. One manufacturer calls them "contemporary" and states that they have "proven convenient and durable in thousands of centers."[32] Another manufacturer calls this kind of cot a "modern playlearn cot" and claims that it "cradles" children. "Ultra space saving compact nesting, and unique built-in channels under child for aeration and draining urine."[33] The catalogs do not state that in all probability the cots will be used in the same rooms where children spend the entire day. Nor does the one with the special aeration and drainage system say where the urine drains and who cleans whatever has drained. It does say "sanitary plastic cots clean instantly with damp cloth."[34] It is ironic that something as lifeless as molded plastic can be called a cradle for a child, when the word *cradle* carries with it connotations of rocking, nurturance, and protection.

Source: Courtesy of Hertz Furniture Systems Co., New York.

Figure 2-5. Modern Playlearn Cots

Source: Courtesy of Childcraft Educ. Corp., Edison, N.J.

Figure 2-6. Contemporary Cot

Another significant indication of our society's view of children, its trend toward dehumanization, is the plastic authorization card. Its manufacturer advertises it as "the ideal way to show parents and guardians that you are sincerely concerned with the added security and safety of their children." It will prevent the unauthorized pickup of children from child-care centers, day nurseries, and other facilities for children. Therefore, its maker claims, "it is an outstanding selling point when comparing the merits of your facility to others in your area." In bold, black letters, the brochure states: "Show them that you care with your very own plastic authorization card."[35] (See figure 2-7.)

But the plastic authorization card may become as necessary for the 1980s as is the plastic credit card; for there is a growing trend to create drop-in, or casual, child-care centers, especially in shopping malls. The plastic card becomes the substitute for the claim checks used by laundries, cleaners, and cobblers. And just as most claim-check stubs state "no merchandise delivered without this check," the authorization card insures proper pick-up. The authorization-card advertisement does not say what contingency plans it recommends for the loss or theft of the parental plastic card.

Another commercial enterprise that seems to blur the lines between nurturing and profit is a chain of day-care centers. The chain recently offered a coupon worth one free day for newly enrolled children. There in the newspaper was the coupon, flanked by ads promising bargains on coffee and detergent purchases. "Enroll now!" the ad said, "where fun and learning go together."

None of these methods or materials has been designed according to principles of child development. Instead, they aim to meet the needs and convenience of adults and add to the profits of manufacturers. Men, women,

Unfortunately, present conditions in our society make it necessary for Day Nurseries, Child Care Centers, Kindergartens, Private Schools, etc. to take certain precautions to guarantee the safety and security of their school children . . . precautions that were not necessary in the past.

A Plastic Authorization Card

- PREVENTS THE UNAUTHORIZED PICK UP OF CHILDREN.
- EMPHASIZES YOUR SCHOOL'S CONCERN WITH THE ADDED SAFETY AND SECURITY OF THE CHILDREN LEFT IN YOUR CARE.
- IS AN OUTSTANDING SELLING POINT WHEN COMPARING THE MERITS OF YOUR FACILITY TO OTHERS IN YOUR AREA.

SHOW THEM THAT YOU CARE

WITH YOUR VERY OWN PLASTIC AUTHORIZATION CARD

PLEASE SEE REVERSE SIDE FOR FREE SAMPLE INFORMATION

Source: Courtesy of Continental Plastic Card Co., Coral Springs, Fla.

Figure 2-7. Plastic Authorization Cards

and the women's movement must accept some of the responsibility for this dehumanizing trend. Those responsible for the manufacture and use of some of these time savers should read the words of the late Dorothy Cohen of the Bank Street College of Education. In 1979, in the International Year of the Child, she wrote "technology in no way substitutes for the particular and special requirements of our children, whose need is not for efficiency and production rates, but to grow into humanness. For them, interaction with people and the natural world is still the road to social, emotional, moral, and intellectual maturing. That road is being bypassed more and more as the criteria for efficient production are applied unthinkingly to the education of children."[36]

3 At the Center

There is a proliferation in the popular press and in the scholarly world of books and articles about children. This wealth of literature intensifies the belief that the United States is a child-centered society. Volume I of the National Day Care Study, conducted by Abt Associates, is a summary of the study's major findings and is titled *Children at the Center.*[1] That title, of course, has a double meaning. It refers to children in day-care centers, and it infers a concentration on, an interest in, a centering on the child.

The entire report of the Abt study is composed of five volumes of statistics, charts, projections, and narrative surveys. It was compiled by a group of social-science researchers who visited 57 sites in Atlanta, Detroit, and Seattle. They did naturalistic recordings of teacher and child behavior, and they administered performance tests to the children. It is, to date, one of the most comprehensive studies of day-care centers in the United States. Another study, which was done in the 1970s by the National Council of Jewish Women, is called *Windows on Day Care.*[2] In that study, volunteers visited 431 day-care centers and family day-care homes in the United States and recorded their observations and interviews. These results were later combined and analyzed by Mary Keyserling, a social-science researcher. Both studies shed light on many of the issues of day care. The Abt study highlighted issues such as class size, teacher child ratio, caregiver education and experience, and child-related training. The National Council Study explored both the positive and negative aspects of day care and called for broad changes in public policy to improve and expand day-care services. But both of these studies share an essential flaw, which is that the researchers visited day-care centers for short amounts of time. Unless one is actually in a day-care center for a period of months, day after day, it is impossible to really know what life at the center is like. Looking through the windows on day care is not the same as experiencing it.

In fact, the only people who spend all day, every day, five days a week, up to fifty-two weeks a year *at the center* are children. Unfortunately, children cannot record their experiences; they cannot write journals or keep anthropological notes. Early childhood is a time when, according to Erik Erikson, children are developing a sense of trust and a concept of autonomy, of personal control and mastery over their environment.[3] Instead, children at the center live in an institutional setting for eight or nine or ten hours a day, often with little control over that environment.

If the children could write notes, thereby articulating their experiences, several things might emerge as significant. They would probably begin by expressing an overwhelming sense of bewilderment, for infants and young toddlers have not yet developed what Piaget calls *object permanence.*[4] They are still cognitively unable to keep an image in their minds of what their mothers look like, and they do not comprehend time. They are, therefore, unable to understand where their mothers are or when they will be back.

The older preschooler might be able to hold images of her mother but still cannot understand what is happening. She begins to wonder why her mother has abandoned her. Because she thinks magically, because she has a primitive sense of cause and effect, and because she believes in her own omnipotence, she wonders if she did something bad to bring about this punishment.[5] Most important, she wonders if her mother will ever come back. The child in day care then experiences, or certainly witnesses, separation anxiety.

Much of the literature on separation is derived from the studies of maternal attachment and deprivation done by Rene Spitz in the 1940s and by John Bowlby in the 1950s and 1960s. The original studies were of institutionalized infants and young children. They indicated that consistent mothering in a stable, stimulating, caretaking environment was essential for the cognitive, physical, and emotional development of the young child.[6]

Bowlby made an interesting contibution to the literature in his construct of the three stages infants experience during hospitalizations, after the sudden departure of their mothers. The first is the *protest stage,* during which the child shows anger by shaking the crib, crying, and thrashing. During the second stage, which Bowlby labeled the *despair stage*, the protests subside and the child becomes sad and passive. During this stage, the child also develops a resentment of the mother and displays anger at any reminder of her. In the final stage, *detachment,* the child becomes less withdrawn than in the despair stage and looks as if she has adjusted. But these despair-stage children show a lack of interest in the mother at reunion time. "Such behavior masks damaging, long-range consequences: in managing to get along without their mothers, the children may sacrifice the ability to sustain enduring relationships with anyone."[7]

Bowlby observed this three-stage pattern of behavior in children from infancy through age four. Other researchers have replicated and refined Bowlby's theories.[8] His theories have been challenged by still others.[9] Nevertheless, most people who work with young children in group settings do not question the theories of separation anxiety, for they frequently witness milder versions of all of the stages that Bowlby describes.

Babies do protest when they are first brought to a group situation and left there. One expert, Dr. Nina Lief, director of the Early Childhood Development Center of New York Medical College, has suggested that if mothers must go back to work, they should make the separation when their infants are about three-months old. She says that by the age of six months, the baby has begun to form a binding attachment to the mother. Also, it is at about this age that the baby develops an awareness of the differences between her mother and herself. Dr. Lief suggests, then, that if the mother separates when the baby is three-months old, the baby will form a meaningful attachment to the caretaker. Dr. Lief advises the mother to create her own pattern of relating to the child so that their attachment becomes more like the father-child attachment.[10] Thus, one way to deal with the protests is to avoid the attachment in the first place.

Toddlers and preschoolers protest also when they first must separate from their mothers. Their protests may be less angry than those of infants, but they are no less poignant. Two-year-old Nicole cried one morning at her day-care center. "I want to go home. I want to go home," she kept repeating. Finally, her mother said to her, "But Nicole, home would be very lonely."

Another child used protest so vehemently that he was withdrawn from a day-care center. The Smiths had been married for ten years and had both achieved professional successes in their childless lives. They thought long and hard before they decided to adopt an interracial child. They also decided to adopt a child who would be old enough to start in day care so that Lynn Smith, a full-time stock analyst, would not have to give up her job. Lynn and Tom did take a two-week vacation for Carlos. Tom flew to Colombia where he picked up the twenty-month-old child and brought him home. The first two weeks were not easy; but, with almost constant attention and care, Carlos began to trust them and to respond happily to them. Then, one day, he was brought to a day-care center. On that first day, his new mother stayed with him and he seemed comfortable for the few hours he was there. On the second day, he was left at the center without his mother for a few hours. He sobbed and was inconsolable. Because he was so disruptive of the routine and because his crying was frightening to the other children, the director took him to her office. He remained inconsolable. She attempted to take him for a walk, but he continued to sob. In sheer exhaustion he finally fell asleep in the director's arms. Carlos behaved in the same way for the next few days, so the director finally asked the parents to withdraw the child. The center did not have adequate staff or space to give Carlos the kind of individual time and attention he was demanding. The parents protested and accused the center of not giving the child a fair chance. But the director and the governing board of the center, made up of other parents, held firm. A month later when the director tried to telephone the Smiths to find out how Carlos was doing, she could get no response from them.

Perhaps the day-care center did fail. Perhaps it should have tried to keep Carlos for several weeks longer. But, perhaps, Dr. Lief's advice should have been followed. If Carlos had been adopted and placed in day care before the age of three months, he would not have had this kind of reaction. He would have made all his separations before he made any attachments.

In recognition of the problems of separation for children, some nursery schools, with the luxury of an academic calendar, have policies in which teachers make home visits before the beginning of school. The visit by the teacher reassures the child of the connection between home and school.

Some nursery-school teachers write brief notes of welcome to their children a week or so before school starts. Although the children must have someone at home read the message, many are thrilled with the idea of receiving mail. And many use the note as a transitional object—a symbol of the continuity and reciprocity of home and school. They bring the note along on the first days of school.

Still other nursery schools encourage parents to spend as many days in the school as are necessary for the child to feel comfortable in the new environment and familiar with the new adults. Furthermore, many stagger the openings of school, so that only a few children attend each day, often for a shortened morning. In other words, children in very small groups are gradually introduced into a new and unfamiliar world. This kind of gradual, caring, reciprocal transition means more security and, some believe, more lasting assurances about school.

Most day-care centers do not have such luxuries. Because of time and energy and salary constraints, day-care teachers cannot be expected to make home visits. Day-care parents cannot always take the time to spend with the child in a new setting. The center usually operates for the entire year, so there is no beginning or end to the year. Children enter when they are old enough, or when there is adequate space, or when their mother gets a job. They do not enter when *their* needs are the major consideration. They do not enter on a staggered schedule or for fewer hours. Caregivers in situations of abrupt separations often witness behavior reminiscent of the Bowlby stages. They see children protest, they see children despair, and they see children become detached.

Desperation and detachment seem present in the case of three-year-old Andrew. He has been in center-based care since he was two. Before that, he was in a family day-care home. He is delivered to the center at eight in the morning and picked up at five o'clock. Andrew's mother is a social worker and she often sees clients late in the day. His father is an engineer and has a long commute to his job. His parents like to get Andrew home at a reasonable hour, so they employ a neighborhood high-school student to pick Andrew up at five o'clock every day and bring him home. On days when the student has conflicts in her schedule, Andrew's grandmother often picks him up.

One day, Andrew was on the playground of his day-care center with a small group of children, all waiting for the five o'clock pickup. "Oh look,

Andrew," said the teacher, "Here comes your mother." Andrew looked at the teacher in surprise and asked, "My real mother?"

The issues of attachment and separation cause some special feelings for the child at the center. But that child experiences other feelings, too. She is beginning to enjoy cooperative play with other children and can sustain it well for a long period of time, perhaps as long as 45 minutes. However, she is in this place not for 45 minutes, but for eight hours, or 480 minutes; sometimes, for some children, for ten hours, or 600 minutes. She must learn how to engage in social interactions for periods of time that would stress the most sociable, gregarious adult—for time spans that are more than ten times what many child-development experts consider exceptionally long for a preschool child. In fact, because of these long hours together, some children in day care develop bickering relationships with one another. They act like some close-in-age siblings, vying for adult attention, competing for materials and equipment, getting on each other's nerves.

The child in day care also begins to become attached to her teachers. But she has to adjust to different styles of teachers because the staff works in shifts. One study found that even in settings with individually assigned caretakers, infants had as many contacts with other adults as they had with their assigned caretakers.[11] For the older child, there are problems also. One teacher might allow the child to put dolls in the water table; another teacher might forbid it. It is not easy to learn rules when the rules are not consistent. Even after the child is familiar with all of her teachers and their rules, there are inconsistencies. For the turnover of staff is higher in day care than in the other human-service professions.[12]

The results of this high rate of turnover were evident when a three-year-old child had a temper tantrum at his day-care center. His teacher could not console him, so she brought him to the director's office. The director held him on her lap and tried to comfort him, but he said that he wanted Kathy. "But Michael," said the director, "Kathy is your afternoon teacher." "Then I want Linda," he said. "Oh Michael, you must remember, Linda teaches in another school now." "Then I want Cheryl." The director chuckled, because Cheryl had been his first teacher at the center, when he was two. "My goodness, Michael, you have a good memory. You remember Linda and you remember Cheryl." And, Michael said, "And I even remember Debby." Debby had been the assistant teacher when he was two. The director realized that the child had had ten major caretakers in two years. They were teachers and assistant teachers and had been special to Michael and had disappeared from his life. The total of ten did not even include student teachers, aides, or volunteers.

Coping with all those different teachers is a difficult task for a young child. But, in all likelihood, the child will also have to do some coping with aggression, either as an aggressor or as a victim. Aggression is present in any preschool setting. Yet in the very comprehensive book, *Day Care, Scientific and Social Policy Issues,* aggression is not even a subject in the index. Instead, in the alphabetical spot where it might be, one finds "aggregate impact model, of child care costs."[13] It is another irony about day care that ignoring the issue of aggression in day care may eventually impact heavily on future aggregate costs to society.

Aggression—an act of hostility or an assault on some one or some thing—is a normal and necessary part of development. Growing up involves learning how to control one's aggressive behavior toward other children and toward adults. The child under three does not have the cognitive or verbal ability to express anger or fear, frustration or concern. She can only express these feelings in physical ways. Part of the responsibility of parents and early-childhood teachers and day-care workers is to help children express their feelings and, simultaneously, gain self-control over their impulses. Until they do so, they often act out, in antisocial ways. It is not until a child is four or five that she can be expected to use language to handle her feelings.

Even then, at four and five, children do not necessarily understand the aggression they witness. Sara, for instance, is an upholder of law and order and a master of cause and effect. She sought a reason for aggression. Her classmate, Anthony, is a difficult four-year-old child. He has been at the center since he was two and has always been an aggressive, angry child. Despite therapy for himself and his parents he continues at four to have an extraordinary temper. He has not learned how to control his aggressive impulses and to express them verbally instead of physically. All of his classmates are very wary of him. They often accuse him of being a bad boy; they claim that they do not want to play with him. Sara is a scientist. She makes logical deductions based on what she has observed in the classroom. She has deduced that Anthony's problem is his name. "If his parents wanted him to be a good boy," she asks, "why did they name him Anthony?"

Exposure to aggression is just one part of the busyness of the day-care day. Because of the constant stimulation, at some point during the day, the child might have need for privacy, for a quiet time and separate space. But because a day-care-center staff must always know where each child is, there can be no actual separate space for a single child. Teachers and environmental planners have done some interesting work with space and equipment. They have constructed lofts with areas that give the illusion of separateness; they have designed quiet corners with cozy, soft sofas; they have created the feeling of small private nooks and crannies. But these spaces are never—or at least never should be—out of the observation and hearing range of the staff. And, although there might be rules about the number of children in one particular space at a time—only three on top of the loft, often so designated by three dots or pictures of three children—an aggressive child can always attempt to join or usurp someone else's space. If the staff/child ratio is a low one, then the teacher probably cannot always protect the privacy of the child who seeks it.

Unfortunately, for some children there might be too much privacy. A director of a day-care center for infants removed all the mobiles from the babies' cribs. She had done an informal study and had noticed that her highly trained staff tended to glance at babies playing with crib mobiles and not go over to them. Children lying in their cribs who paid no attention to their mobiles received more attention from the teachers. In other words, babies who ignored their mobiles were picked up more frequently than those who played with them. After long and anguishing thought, the director decided that it was best for the children to miss the stimulation of the crib toys as a trade-off for more valuable, individual, physical attention.

Another critical issue for the child at the center is the issue of role models. Some of the research on day care has shown that children in day care are more peer-oriented. They do not seek the help of adults as much as home-raised children do.[14] If a child in a day-care center sees her peers as her major models, she sees behavior that parents might want to discourage. She sees aggression. She sees anger. She sees fear. She sees disruptive conduct. She sees passivity. Children do learn from each other, but they also learn from adults. And they learn from their own experience. What they see they tend to incorporate into their own behaviors. In the day-care center they see mostly children.

The adult models in the day-care center can be appropriate or inappropriate, but those models are generally women. Children in day-care centers see women teachers and assistants, women cooks and social workers. If the most common model in a center is a child, the next most common model is a female. And, it is important, though sad, to emphasize that many of these females are not satisfied with their work. Therefore, in large numbers of cases, the female adult model is a depressed or unhappy model. Many contemporary parents, some of whom consider themselves feminists, emphasize the importance of nonstereotyped role models. And then, they enroll their children in institutions where, all too frequently, depressed women do what is perceived as menial work. The role model of the successful woman in the gray flannel suit with the leather briefcase does not work at the day-care center.

For boys at the center it is even harder. They often see no males at all, with the exception of an occasional janitor. In the course of an ordinary day, they do not see bus drivers or firemen, male teachers or supermarket-shelf stackers. Nor do they see men nurturing small children. The number of male teachers in day care is so negligible that the stereotypical role of woman as caretaker is reinforced.

Children, of course, cannot describe their day at the center. They cannot take notes on separation or aggression. They cannot comment about high staff turnover or stereotypical role models. Nor can they discuss the actual physical environment. Yet the physical environment of the day-care center is a critical influence on the behavior and development of both children and staff.

The first requisite for the environment is that it is safe for young children. Safety means that there can be no lead paint in the building. It means that there must be accessible fire exits. It means that there must be adequate heating and ventilation and toilet facilities. The second requisite, after safety, is space. Requirements for sufficient space vary from state to state, but the minimum recommendation is thirty-five square feet of unencumbered space per child. Fifty square feet is preferable.[15] Once those two very measurable requirements are met, the use of space depends on the center budget and the goals and skills of its staff and parents. Early-childhood educators have long worked on defining the components of the environment that make for the most cooperative, industrious, child-enriching, productive programs. They recommend that spaces be subdivided into interest and activity areas. Each area, although it must be visible to the adults, can be defined by the placement of bookcases or room dividers.

Space must be attractive to the children and responsive to their needs. Therefore, each classroom should have some open space and some more closed, intimate space. It should have soft space with carpeting, cushions, or upholstered furniture, and it should have hard space with bare floors for creative movement and block building. It should have high space and low space. The high space is important for the sheer physical activity of climbing, for the satisfaction of being bigger or taller than others, for a relief from the monotony, and for a place to feel some privacy sometimes. The low spaces serve as contrasts to the high places and offer similar opportunities for privacy.

A day-care center should have child space and teacher space. Because space is an important cost for centers and because centers must operate at full capacity, it is often difficult for them to provide adequate teacher space. There are frequently no separate places that can be set aside as teachers' rooms, for rest and relaxation. In most cases, teachers must use the office for that kind of space. The office is not just the administrative and clerical center. It is also frequently the first-aid station and the isolation space for sick children. It is often the only place where conferences with parents or consultants can be held with any modicum of confidentiality. If it is the place for teachers' rest and relaxation, it is clear that, in the course of their day, teachers have as little privacy as the children do.

Another problem presented by the lack of spacious facilities is storage. In any given day-care center, there are—on top of shelves and cupboards and tucked into unused corners but still quite visible—numerous supermarket shopping bags and cardboard cartons. They contain what nursery-school teachers call beautiful junk: egg cartons and toilet-paper rolls; plastic containers and oatmeal boxes; styrofoam noodles and fabric scraps. It is interesting that most homes do not store their trash out in the open. But aesthetic standards for homes are quite different than those for day-care centers, despite the fact that many children who attend day care full-time spend more waking hours there than they do in their own homes.

Still another problem with space, and one that adds to the complexities of the day-care issue, is that space must be used for multiple purposes. Thus,the table used for art activity is also used for eating. The sponges used to clean that art/eating table are often also used for wiping up spills from the floor. The teachers, no matter what the ratio, do not have the necessary time to enforce use of separate sponges or to insist that each sponge gets thoroughly cleaned after each use. Surely this is one of the reasons for some of the health problems associated with day-care centers. Filled to capacity and short-staffed, centers are difficult to keep neat and orderly, let alone hygienic.

In fact, at one center with nine two-year olds and two teachers, the staff cannot leave the classroom long enough to help all the children with their toileting. In the classroom, in the room where they eat and play and sleep, there is a changing table and a diaper pail for those children still in diapers.[16] Next to the changing table, on the floor, there are two small potties. Those children who are already potty trained use those potties. When each child is finished, she must carry her potty basin to the bathroom, empty it, rinse it with a small spray attached to the water faucet and return it to its place in the room for the next child to use. It is no wonder that germs and viruses spread to both children and adults. This particular center is in an affluent suburban community and it is licensed by both the state and local licensing agencies. It serves professional parents and their children.

Multiple use of space also means some problems with naps. In most homes, there are separate sleeping facilities. That is, children do not play, eat, and sleep in the same room. It is also true that in most homes people use the same bed each night, and that bed is in the same place each night. However, few day-care centers can afford a separate nap room. Therefore, cots are piled up in a corner of the room used for playing, working, and eating, and are brought down for naps. Now it becomes the play-work-eat-sleep room. If there are adequate staff members they can guarantee that each child gets the same spot and the same cot each day. But if it is an overworked, harassed staff, then the easiest and quickest thing to do, is to put out the cots and, as the children are ready for their naps, have them take a cot.

Sleep and dreams often present a problem for children and for parents, for they are a time of fear and confusion for many children. When children have sleep disturbances, one of the first things suggested to parents is consistency. "Be firm," the experts say, "about when and where the child sleeps. Reassure the child that she will be safe, that she will be comforted for any bad dreams she might have, and that she will get help if she needs a drink or must go to the bathroom." It seems unlikely that that kind of firmness and consistency can be conveyed to the child in a situation where she is not even in the same place each day and where there are competing children, some of whom may be crying, some of whom may be coughing, and all of whom are undoubtedly in need of individual attention.

In some day-care centers, not all children sleep. Arrangements are made for older children and those who require less sleep to do quiet activities in a room separated from the nappers. In fact, there are parents who request that their children not be allowed to sleep. "If she naps," one set of parents told the teacher, "then we have her up half the night." In another center, a mother was told that her child, usually a nonsleeper, had in fact slept that day. "Well, Peter," said his mother, "you didn't get much out of this afternoon's program, did you?" The mother's message, to both the child and the teacher, was that sleep was not an appropriate activity for a young child.

Ordinary nap times at day-care centers can present problems for children and for staff and for parents; but, there are also unusual nap times. Fire drills during naps provide an example of what happens at unusual times. All institutions need to have fire drills to ensure that the occupants of a building can get to safety in a reasonably short amount of time. Fire drills for young children always present some difficulties. Teachers explain the reasons for and the procedures of a fire drill. They tell the children that they are just practicing. They try to reassure children that the idea does not give way to the reality, that having a pretend drill will not actually cause a fire. But, even children as old as four are convinced that there is actually a fire at their center when it is only a fire drill. Fire drills become, then, a scary, though necessary, part of group living. A well-run center wants to make sure that a staff is able to function quickly in an emergency at any time of the day, so it often has fire drills during nap times. Researchers and policymakers who recommend eight- or ten-to-one ratios[17] should—without any other adults—try to empty a nap room of that many sleeping children, especially while a fire inspector watches with a stopwatch. Some of the children have a hard time waking up; they just turn over and go right back to sleep. Some want to go to the bathroom. Some insist on taking their blankets with them. Some cry because they are frightened and think it is a real fire. These same researchers and policymakers should then try to put the eight or ten children back to sleep or attempt to keep them happy and occupied for the rest of the day.

What the teacher might do after that kind of traumatic event is take the children outdoors for the rest of the day, if the weather permits it—for the playground is also part of the day-care environment. Massachusetts Rules and Regulations for Day Care Centers require seventy-five square feet of fenced-in outdoor space per child.[18] Early-childhood educators view the outdoors as an extension of the indoors. Therefore, it is a place where children continue to need help in their growth and development, particularly in social and physical development. Material and equipment and space should be available for climbing and running, for wheel toys and sand play. Teachers must be alert to help children in these areas and, of course, for accident prevention—but that does not always happen.

On a hot and humid day in August a teacher in a middle-class day-care center took a sick day. Her assistant was given responsibility for a class of fifteen children, with a junior-high-school volunteer aide. The assistant teacher was a single parent whose salary, plus food stamps and subsidized housing, was not enough to support her young son and herself. She was associated with a local rock-music group and often sang with them to earn extra money. She had had a successful but late "gig" the night before that humid day and, consequently, was quite tired. When it was time to go outdoors, she asked the aide to wash the paint brushes before joining the group on the playground.

Then the exhausted assistant teacher went out to the playground with the fifteen children and sat in the shade while the children went to their various activities: sand box, swings, slide, jungle gyms. She leaned against the tree and, like the peddler in the children's classic *Caps for Sale*,[19] fell sound asleep. When the young volunteer came out to the playground, she was unsure about what to do. Afraid to antagonize the assistant teacher, she did not dare to wake her. Yet she was frightened of the responsibility she had for fifteen children. The children, with their uncanny intuition, sensed what was happening and began to get out of control. Their noise awakened the assistant teacher, which was probably their unconscious, unarticulated goal to begin with.

The head teacher was back the next day, but the assistant said nothing about her nap. It took several days for the volunteer to summon up enough courage to tell the head teacher what happened on the playground. The head teacher in turn reported the incident to the director. The director had overlooked other infringements by that particular assistant because of her affection and compassion for her. But now, she felt, she had to request a resignation.

Policy analysts see licensing as one means to guarantee safe, quality care for children. But licensing varies from state to state. Adult-child ratios are one example of the variety in licensing. Arizona law allows one adult to care for as many as ten children under age two. Both Ohio and South Carolina allow eight infants to one adult, while Florida permits six infants to one adult. Florida allows a ratio of one adult to twelve three-year olds and a ratio of one to twenty for four-to-five-year olds. It would seem impossible for workers with those ratios to evacuate for a fire drill, let alone for a real fire. Conversely, it would seem possible that the fatigue would be so overwhelming to caregivers that some might feel entitled to steal a quick nap on the playground.

According to *The Federal Interagency Day Care Requirements* (FIDCR), "there is no assurance that state and local safety and sanitation codes adequately protect the well-being of the child in the day-care environment."[20] And, if licensing cannot protect the well-being of the child, then it certainly cannot guarantee quality. Licensing is limited by many of the same budgetary restrictions that apply to all human services. Agencies cannot afford enough well-trained licensors. Once a licensor has a heavy case load, it is almost impossible to monitor all the centers. The licensor must work on an appointment basis with centers and so cannot make essential surprise visits.

Even when the licensing agency knows of infringements, huge problems are created if it attempts to close down a facility. There are problems for the staff and problems for the parents. Therefore, most licensing agencies try to work with the facility to help it improve its services. Like so much connected with day care, it is often a thankless and frustrating job. "I spend my life," said one licensor, "in church basements."

Jay Belsky, Laurence Steinberg, and Ann Walker in "The Ecology of Day Care," speak of the importance of the local supervisory agency in assuring quality care:

> A day care center was . . . closed down on short notice when its lease was not renewed. In many . . . communities such an event would surely have wreaked havoc on a large number of families. This was not the case, however, because the local child development council was responsible for overseeing center as well as family day care programs. Thus, a large number of children were smoothly transferred from the to-be-closed center program to FDC (Family Day Care) home programs that were either already in operation or quickly established to handle this situation. Except for the change in the locale of day care, parents were minimally inconvenienced by what was a rather radical disruption in the availability of day care services.[21]

In this example a judgment of *quality* is awarded because of minimal inconvenience to parents. No mention is made of the possible trauma to children that an abrupt change can generate. No mention is made of the child having to readjust to a new physical environment and to a new caretaker. No mention is made of the compromising that might have been made to quickly establish new programs. And, of course, no mention is made about what became of the day-care staff in the center whose lease was not renewed!

One unusual, but frightening, example of the limits of licensing happened in a middle-class, suburban day-care center. Jennifer was a dental assistant who was also taking evening courses in early-childhood education at the local community college. She took the courses for two reasons: she had always thought that she might like to work in a day-care center someday; and she felt that the community-college courses would eventually help her to become a better mother. One of her course assignments was to visit a day-care center. That assignment was not an easy one for someone taking night courses; most of the students had jobs and had a hard time getting the few hours off they needed to make their visits. Finally, Jennifer managed to arrange an afternoon off to do her center visit. She made an appointment at a licensed, proprietary facility in the town where the community college was located. She arrived and found one woman with twelve three- and four-year olds. The woman said, "Oh, I'm so glad you've come. I've run out of crackers and have to get some." Jennifer said, "What?" And the woman, who was the owner of the center, said, "I'll just be gone for a few minutes. I'll be right back." Jennifer replied, "I'm sorry, but I can't stay here with all of these children." And the owner said, "Oh, sure you can." The woman then walked out the door without even saying good-bye to the children.

Jennifer almost burst into tears. She did not know the names of the children. She did not know the limits of the classroom. She did not even know exactly how many children were there. She went to the telephone but realized that she didn't even know whom to call. She wished that she knew how to reach her class instructor.

After fifteen minutes of chaos for the children and anguish for Jennifer, the owner director did come back. Jennifer left, still in a state of shock. At the next class meeting she reported the incident to her instructor. Together, Jennifer and the instructor reported the incident to the local licensing agency, which said it would handle the matter. The next time Jennifer and her teacher heard about the center was six months later. Its license had been changed to accommodate more children.

It is clear that children cannot articulate what their day-care experience is like. Researchers see only a small portion of it. Licensing agencies, too, are limited in what they witness and what they can correct. Teachers and other staff, although not usually at the center for the entire day, from opening to closing, sometimes can give the most honest and perceptive appraisals of what life actually is like at the center.

Some day-care teachers find early morning the hardest time. As children begin to arrive, they are sometimes cranky, sometimes quite whiney with their parents. Parents, in turn, often justifiably tired and harassed, sometimes feel guilt about leaving the child and that ambivalence, communicated unconsciously to the child, is scary for her. She thinks, also unconsciously: If my parents have doubts about this place, maybe it isn't a safe place to be. And so the parent and the child begin a charade of not being able to say good-bye to each other.

Often, the earliest morning shift at the day-care center is made up of just one teacher, and so the adult greeting the child and the parent may not even be the child's actual classroom teacher or primary caretaker. Because time is so limited for the adults working at the center, there are not sufficient opportunities for the staff to spend discussing each child. So, the early morning teacher on a particular morning—the one who must greet and help in the transition from home to school—may not know what techniques are best for reassuring that particular parent and child.

Other day-care teachers find the end of the day the hardest. Children are tired. They have had up to ten hours of group living and it is a strain. They have noticed that some of their friends left earlier, at three o'clock. Of course, they do not have the cognitive ability to understand time. Ten minutes to an anxious child can seem like an eternity. When a child asks, "When will my mommy come?" and the teacher says, "Soon," the word has no substantial meaning. As Anna Freud has pointed out in "The Emotional and Social Development of Young Children," "all young children have a time sense very different from our own. . . . We treat the child on the basis of our time sense, when we should treat him on the basis of his own time sense."[22]

Because there are fewer numbers of children at the end of the day, once again in the interests of budgets, there is reduced staff for the last hour or so. Just as some children are greeted in the early morning by someone other than their head teacher, others must spend the last anxious hour with a different teacher.

In one New England center, where it gets dark early in the winter months, children wait from about five to six each evening in the coziest room at the center. The only problem with that room is that it is beyond double doors, at the end of a hall with tiled floors. Parents arriving after dark can be heard opening the door and walking down the hall. The last four or five children there each day stop all noise at the first sound of the double doors opening and the footsteps. Children as young as two-and-a-half are able to recognize the walks of the various parents. A quiet child might be working on a puzzle and say, wistfully, "Oh, Danny, it's your mom."

Still other teachers find emergency situations the hardest part of life at the center. One day-care center closed officially at six o'clock. Because some parents ignored the clock and were often late, the center had a policy of charging five dollars for every fifteen-minute block of time that parents were late. The five dollars was not added to the center budget, but went directly to the teacher who stayed beyond her regular working hours.

On one particular day, Sam's mother did not come at six. Sue, the teacher on late duty, felt badly. She was exhausted, and she knew that

Sam's mother could ill afford the late fine. Sam's mother and father had been having a terrible time and the father finally left and disappeared. Sue tried to reassure Sam that everything was okay, his mother had probably had a flat tire. She tried to interest him in a story, but he insisted on standing at the window and waiting. They waited and waited. Sue called her roommate to tell her why she was late and kept trying to reach Sam's mother at her home and at her place of business, but she kept getting no answer. At seven, she finally called the director of the center at her home, fifteen miles away. Luckily, the director had just attended a workshop on the legal aspects of day care and had learned that in their state, if the teacher left the premises with the child, she would first have to do several things. She would have to notify the local police that she was doing so; she would have to post a sign on the door of the building telling where she was taking the child; and she would have to go to the child's home and post a sign on that door also informing the parents where the child had been taken. She had also learned that if parents could not be traced, then the police would take the child to the local hospital.

Neither Sue nor the director had space for the child in their homes and neither could spend the night at the center. They called a friend of Sam's mother who volunteered to take Sam, although she had no car and could not come to get him. Sue delivered Sam to that house and then went around posting signs. The center learned the next day that the mother had had a ruptured appendix at work and had been taken to the emergency room of the local hospital. Someone at work was supposed to notify the center but in the midst of the emergency had forgotten.

There are, then, ordinary days and unusual days for staff women and for children at the center. But, it appears that at all times children's needs are not at the core; they are not central to the day-care experience. Instead, the needs of adults—of parents and employers and policymakers—take precedence over the needs of children at the center. "The world in which children live—the institutional world that babies, toddlers, and the very young have increasingly come to inhabit and confront—is a world in which they have become the objects, not the subjects of history, a world in which *history is being made of them* (italics in original)."[23]

4 A Day in the Life of Ivy Denison

Ivy Denison arrives at her day-care center at 8:00 in the morning. Her father drops her off because her mother, a teacher, goes to work a half hour earlier. She carries a tote bag. Because no lunch is served at her center, she has a lunch box and a thermos in the tote bag. Because she got her clothes wet the day before when working at the water table and had to wear the extra change of clothes kept at school, she has another replacement change of clothing. Because the teachers are planning a field trip next week and need parental permission slips, she has the signed slip in her tote bag; she thinks that if she loses that slip, she won't be able to go to the zoo. Because she is three, she has a teddy bear and a book in the tote bag. At 8:00 in the morning she is carrying a tote bag along with considerable responsibility for its contents.

Her father helps her remove her jacket, put the clothing change in her shoe box, and put her lunch box and thermos on the shelf of her cubby. There is only a small refrigerator at the center, so her lunch box remains in the cubby all morning. The grapes she loves to eat for dessert never taste as good as they do at home because they are never cold enough. She tries to put her book into her shoe box, because the shoe box is actually the only absolutely private space she will have for the next eight hours. Oh, yes, the cubby is hers, but it is open and its contents can be seen by all the children and the teachers. But, the book will not fit in the shoe box, so she asks her father to put it on top of the cubby. When he does, he finds on the top of her cubby one red rubber with no identification on it and a small plastic truck with three wheels. He asks Ivy if they are hers and she says, "No." The rubber belongs to Matthew, the truck to Laura. Just as she carries responsibility for the contents of the tote bag, she carries responsibility for other people's possessions.

After about five minutes of dealing with these practical matters, Ivy and her father go into the classroom. The teachers at Ivy's center alternate the early shift, and this week the early morning teacher is Ruth, the toddler teacher. Ivy is always happy when Ruth is the early morning teacher. Ivy remembers Ruth from her own toddler days and so feels very comfortable with her. The hardest mornings are when the head teacher of the fours is there. She is new to the center and Ivy hardly knows her.

Ruth has put out some pegs and puzzles at one table and some playdough at another. Ivy goes to the puzzles and shows her father how well she can do the Raggedy Ann one. After about five more minutes, he says that he really must leave. He kisses her good-bye and reminds her that her mother will be picking her up in the afternoon. She continues to work on the puzzles as more children arrive. Some are toddlers; some are threes and fours; and some are five-year olds who will later go to the afternoon session of the local public kindergarten. More teachers also begin to arrive and take their assigned children to their assigned rooms. When Jane, Ivy's teacher, comes in, Ivy gets up from her chair. "No," says Jane, "you need to finish that puzzle so someone else can use it." Ivy is afraid that if she spends too long on that puzzle, Jane will go to the three-year-old class without her. She really wants to go with Jane. So she tries to hurry through the puzzle but can't get it right. She sees that Jane's attention is elsewhere, so she leaves the puzzle undone. She has a conflict between wanting to please Jane by obeying her and wanting to be with Jane. The need for the security of Jane's physical presence wins out. It is now 8:30 in the morning.

When Ivy gets to her own classroom, she asks Jane if Jane will read the book she brought in. Jane says, "Of course, Ivy, remind me at group time." Group time is two hours away. Safe and secure in her own classroom, Ivy and her friend Jay begin to play with blocks. They are both good block builders and they often start the day there, before there are more children with whom to share space and blocks. They work hard building a house and put some wooden block people in it: a mother, a father, a girl, a boy, and a genderless baby. As they stand surveying their work with pride, Tom, a classmate, zooms into the room and kicks over their house. They both yell at Tommy, call out for Jane, and chase Tommy out of the block corner. Jane is busy at the art table so Sandy, the assistant, comes over and helps Ivy and Jay rebuild their house. It is 9:00 A.M.

At 9:00, Jane calls all the children together for a morning meeting. They sing a greeting song and then she tells them the kinds of activities that are available that day. She discusses what they had for breakfast. In that discussion she learns that one child had no breakfast and one had a bag of corn chips. She decides she'd better serve an early snack. She reminds the children about all their choices: water and sand play; house corner; puzzles; playdough. She assures them that if there is no room at their first choice when they get there, they will have a turn later. They discuss who is absent and why; whose mothers and fathers are out of town and why; and finally she reminds Tommy that he must remember to follow the rules of the school. It is 9:20.

Ivy decides that she wants to work at the water table again today. She goes over and puts her hand and arm in. Sandy rushes over and reminds her to roll up her sleeves and helps her put on an apron so she won't have to have another change of clothing today. Ivy is working happily at the water table, pouring water from large containers to small and back again. She works with some of the "sink-float" toys and keeps trying to sink a cork. She is busy with that endeavor when John, next to her at the water table, makes a big splash and Ivy gets water in her eye. Although there's no soap in the water today, it does sting and Ivy cries a little and shouts at John to watch what he is doing. Sandy comes over, pats Ivy on the back, and encourages her to resume her play at the water table, but Ivy says, "No." It is 9:30.

Ivy pats a pet rabbit on her way to the art area and settles in there with some interesting collage material. She makes two collages and is enjoying chitchatting with her friend Elizabeth, but more children approach the table. Since space is limited, Jane says that Ivy will have to give her space to someone after she makes her third collage. She and Elizabeth are cooperative about giving up their spaces and they run over to the house corner holding hands. "You need to walk," says Jane. The girls play together with dishes and pots and pans until 10:00, when the teachers remind the children that it is time to clean up for snack and group. Ivy and Elizabeth clean up their own area and help the teachers pick up the block corner and clean the art tables. Ivy and Elizabeth use a sponge for the collage table and try to scrub the glue that someone had dripped on the table surface. They help pass paper napkins and paper cups, they take their seats at the table and drink juice and eat crackers. The ratio of staff to children in the group is one to seven, so Ivy and six other children eat at the table with Jane. They talk about the weather and about the pet rabbit and about the collages they made that morning. Ivy suddenly remembers her book and begins to get up. "Please stay at the table until you've finished your snack, Ivy," says Jane. Ivy says, "But my book!" and Jane says, "Book? What book, Ivy?" In the confusion of this very ordinary morning Jane, a caring and concerned teacher, has forgotten about Ivy's book. As soon as she says, "What book?" she realizes her mistake and apologizes to Ivy. "Of course, I will read it." It is 10:15.

The children throw their cups and napkins away. Some miss the basket but don't bother to pick up from the floor. Jane gathers them all together for their group time. Ivy rushes to her cubby; her book is not there. She asks a passing adult to check the high shelf above the cubbies, but the book isn't there, either. She runs into the classroom, and Jane, sensing something is wrong, does not say, "You need to walk when you're inside." Jane hears Ivy's report of the missing book but cannot leave the other thirteen children to help her. She asks her assistant, Sandy, to help Ivy find her book. They look in Ivy's tote bag, but the book isn't there. They go to the other classrooms, but no one has seen it. They go to the office, thinking that perhaps someone thought it was lost. Sandy asks Ivy if she is sure that she brought the book today. Ivy begins to cry. Sandy comforts her and finally convinces her to take her teddy bear and go back to the group; they will find the book later. Ivy sits on Sandy's lap during the stories, holding her bear and sucking her thumb. She doesn't participate in the finger plays that Jane and the other children do. Jane begins leading the children in a participation song, and all the children are supposed to stand up. When they do, Ivy's book miraculously appears. Tommy had been sitting on it. Jane and Sandy both scold Tommy. Although Jane thought this activity was going to be the last part of the group time, she decides that Ivy needs the comfort of having her story read. But the other children are quite restless and itchy. Finally, Jane tells them that those who do not want to hear the rest of the story can leave with Sandy; she will read it to any who stay. Ivy and Elizabeth are the only ones who remain. But when Elizabeth sees that Sandy is taking the other children outdoors, she gets up to leave also. Ivy is alone with Jane and Jane finishes the story. It is 11:00.

Jane and Ivy go outside, but Ivy sulks when she sees that all the swings and tricycles are being used. "Want to play in the sand box?" asks Jane. "No," says Ivy. "Jungle gym?" "No." "Slide?" "No." Ivy stands near Jane and follows her when she moves. Ivy is still sulking when she sees Grace walking toward the playground. Grace is one of her afternoon teachers. She rushes over to Grace and hugs her legs. She tells Grace what Tommy did with her book and Grace sympathizes and says, "Oh, that must have been very sad." Grace and Ivy chat for a few minutes, but Grace and Jane need to talk about some important things so they urge Ivy to find something to do. Now that she is outside, where running is permissible, Ivy walks in a slow saunter to the swings, where she asks Sandy for a push. It is 11:15. Ivy finally gets a turn on the tricycles, plays in the sand, and gets into some active running games with some of the other children. She witnesses a terrible fight between Tommy and her friend Jay and sees Sandy take Tommy indoors for what the teachers call time-outs for Tommy. She sees her friend Laura fall off a ladder and bump her head. Grace takes Laura in for first aid. Finally, at noon, Jane gathers the children and brings them inside. Ivy takes off her jacket and goes to the bathroom to get washed. The bathroom is crowded and she cannot get near the paper towels, so she wipes her hands on her blue jeans and gets her lunch box from her cubby. Suddenly she remembers her book and rushes into the classroom to find her book on top of a pile in the story corner. She takes her book and her lunch box to the table and sees a spot of collage glue and cracker crumbs from snack on the table. She opens her lunch box herself but needs adult help with her thermos. Elizabeth sits on one side of her and Ivy says she wants Sandy on the other side. But Jay comes over and says he wants to sit there, so she agrees. She sits at a table with six children, six open lunch boxes, six thermos bottles, and varying amounts of wax paper, plastic wrap, and cellophane. She enjoys her lunch, although she shares some of it with her friends. Today she has carrot sticks and she trades a few for some M&Ms. She complains that her mother never gives her M&Ms in her lunch. All of a sudden she hears John swearing. He is at the other table, so she has to turn around on her chair to see him. He has spilled his milk and it is all over his lunch and his pants. Jane takes care of him and Ivy returns to her lunch and her friends. As the children finish lunch, they take their lunch boxes, some full of crumbs and spilled liquid, back to their cubbies and return to the room where Grace has begun putting out the cots and blankets. Some days, when there is enough time, Jane or Sandy or Grace try to wash everyone's face, but that doesn't seem to be happening today. Ivy looks for her blanket, the one with a picture of Bo-Peep on it, and finds it on a cot in the block corner. On most days, that is where Ivy's cot is, near the blocks and next to Jay's and Elizabeth's cots. But on some days, when they need to have some of the toddlers or some of the fours in their room, Ivy's cot is placed in another part of the room, next to children whom she doesn't really know. She likes it best in the block corner. She lies there with her teddy bear and her book and her blanket and falls asleep with Jane sitting on a nearby chair. It is 12:45.

When Ivy wakes up at 2:30, a teacher named Paula is in the room. Jane and Sandy have left for the day. Grace has been working with the nonsleepers in another room. Paula is the fifth adult other than her parents that Ivy has had to rely on today. She is the eighth that Ivy has talked to; for in her search for her lost book, she talked to the teacher of the fours and to the director and the secretary.

Paula comforts Ivy, reassures her, and tries to ease her confusion. She even offers to read her a story in a quiet whispering voice, but Ivy says, "No, I am thirsty." "Well," says Paula, "snacks are in the other room." Ivy goes into the other room where Grace is working with the already-awake children. Ivy sits down, has some juice, and gradually wakes up. At 2:45 Jay's mother comes to get him. Ivy asks Grace when her own mother is coming. "Soon," says Grace. After her snack, Ivy plays with playdough and talks to Elizabeth and Grace. When Paula sees that all the children are now awake, the class goes outdoors again. Most of the morning playground routine is repeated. Children play actively; they play cooperatively and they have disputes. They play alone and they play in groups. They have minor falls and spills and on occasion serious accidents. On good days, and in good weather, the teachers are apt to keep Ivy and her friends outdoors for several hours. But on this particular day, it is rather cloudy and the children seem to be getting into a lot of fights, so Grace and Paula bring the children in at 3:30. Much of the same kinds of activities are available in the afternoon as were available in the morning: blocks and dolls; puzzles and playdough; music and art. Ivy doesn't feel like doing any of those things. She asks Grace to read her her book. Grace is too busy, but Paula says she will. Paula begins to read the book when an altercation occurs on the other side of the room and Grace is unable to attend to it. Paula must abandon Ivy to resolve the fight. Ivy goes to her cubby and sits in it to wait for her mother. At 4:00 Ivy's mother appears, exhausted from a hard day. She greets Ivy with a big and cheerful hug and Ivy tries to explain what happened when Tommy hid her book. Her mother says, "Well, Ivy, I told you that you should keep that book at home." Ivy opens her tote bag and finds the permission slip for the zoo trip. She has forgotten to give it to Jane! Now she won't be able to go to the zoo. Ivy bursts into tears. Ivy ends her day-care center day in the same way she began it: feeling overwhelming responsibility for her possessions, indeed her life.

Ivy leaves the day-care center at 4:00, but she has friends who stay until 6:00. They spend the last few hours in various ways. In a well-run center, the afternoon teachers might have activities to interest the children but not overstimulate them. They must plan activities that will interest children but ones that they can leave easily, because the tired parent coming to pick up his or her child does not want to wait until the child finishes an activity. The tired parent still has lots of work ahead and wants to leave as soon as possible—for now is when parents must give what some experts call quality time.

5 Staff: In Loco Parentis

Day care is an institution that demands of its staff a two-fold, paradoxical role: professional and menial. Raise our children, parents ask, according to the best theories of Freud, Erikson, and Piaget. Make them healthy, secure, intelligent, challenged, social, happy, ambitious, talented, gentle, competent, loving, independent, and mature. While you are doing that, please change their diapers, toilet train them, keep track of their stray socks and their lost teddy bears. Accept them at your center with upset stomachs and runny noses. If the janitor doesn't show up, please sweep the floors and clean the potties and take out the garbage. Accept my apologies if I am a half hour late. But please don't ever charge me more than two dollars an hour.

Parents certainly wish the best for their children and are sincere about those wishes. But often they cannot give it themselves, nor can they afford to purchase the best for what it is actually worth. And so, in innocence and ignorance, they expect day-care providers to do the best. Be nanny and nurse, cook and teacher, friend and grandmother, disciplinarian and warm lap, musician and artist, psychiatrist and supervisor of outdoor play.

Skeptics say that women have always done these things. And that point is important. Some women have been liberated from traditional roles. But because someone in every society must perform certain jobs, there has actually been a transfer of roles from one group of exploited women—mothers—to another group of exploited women—day-care staff. Some women have entered the operating rooms of hospitals, the boardrooms of banks, courts of law and advertising agencies, computer companies and department stores. Other women have entered day-care centers.

Richard Ruopp and Jeffrey Travers, in "Janus Faces Day Care: Perspectives on Quality and Cost," extrapolated the 1977 figures from the National Day Care Study to 1981 figures. They report that more than half of all center-based caregivers earn less than $3.75 per hour. The actual average wage is estimated to be $3.60 per hour, lower than the U.S. Department of Labor designated poverty line. Fifty-four percent of caregivers have completed some postsecondary education. In fact, Ruopp and Travers report that caregivers have an average of nearly fourteen years of schooling and are, therefore, in the fiftieth percentile in terms of education. But their earnings put caregivers in the lowest 5 percent for all workers. Ruopp and Travers add that head teachers in day-care centers earn approximately half the amount of teachers in public schools.[1]

According to Marcy Whitebook et al., in "Who's Minding the Child Care Workers?," their study of workers in San Francisco showed that day-care workers were among the lower 10 percent of all adult wage earners. Half received no medical coverage and 16 percent had no sick leave.[2] Another survey of twenty-two Minneapolis day-care centers, done by the Childcare Workers' Alliance, indicated that eight centers paid sick-leave benefits. Only two had paid vacations and one had retirement benefits.[3]

Whitebook's study also found that the turnover rate for center staff is 15 to 20 percent as opposed to 10 percent for most workers in the human-service field. As the National Day Care Study found, lower wages were predictive of higher staff turnovers.[4]

Whitebook also found that about a third of the caregivers were from ethnic minorities. Most, of course, were women. This figure was confirmed by another survey of centers in Illinois and New England done by Edgar Klugman and Lana Hostetler. They found that 93 percent of the individuals who responded to their survey were female. Among 153 centers responding, 61 percent reported entirely female staffs, while only 18 percent reported having two or more male staff in direct service to children.[5]

It is another irony of day care that caregivers are in the fiftieth educational percentile and yet are so poorly paid. This discrepancy occurs because they are perceived as unskilled. And, they are seen as unskilled because raising children has traditionally been women's work, and as such, it has not been valued in our culture. If women can do it, anyone can. Perhaps the most blatant proof of that perception has come from the Oval Office. "What better solution," Ronald Reagan asked, "than working mothers drop their kids off at the church, and there are volunteers to take care of them, and there would be no government involved."[6] He also said that mothers and grandmothers have been raising children for centuries, so there is no reason to insist on educational standards for day-care teachers.[7] In fact, mothers and grandmothers were raising children in small numbers, not in large groups. They had an age range of infants and toddlers and older children. And, they had biological limits to the numbers they dealt with. Another important difference between traditional child rearing and day care is that presumably the mothers and grandmothers Reagan talked about *loved* the children they were raising. They were not providing care as a job or a profession or a career. Therefore, they were not concerned with issues of status and professionalism and salary and fringe benefits. An analogy ought to be made to the president that mothers and grandmothers have also been cooking and baking for generations. Therefore, the White House ought to make do with a volunteer chef.

Sensitive professionals, perhaps unintentionally, also undermine the value of child care. Edward Zigler and Jody Goodman recommend the use of high-school students and the elderly as caregivers when children and parents become ill.[8] Alison Clarke-Stewart makes a similar suggestion for the use of teens and senior citizens and proposes that they could work as "house-helpers" or "family aides."[9] Even the author of a most sensitive book about the problems of the working mother, Sheila Kamerman, in *Parenting in an Unresponsive Society*, calls family day care and teacher aide "low-skilled work." Yet elsewhere in the book, a young mother is quoted as saying, "The woman who takes care of Linda is just great with kids but she's so good that everyone wants her and she can't say no. She has between fifteen and twenty-four children in her home on any given day and . . . that's really too many for her to manage alone."[10]

Perhaps if child care were valued more—were not considered low-skilled work but a profession—then family-day-care women like Linda's caretaker would not be in business. Or, if they were superb with children, they would be reimbursed suitably for their hard work, talents, and skills. They would not be forced to take in fifteen to twenty-four children.

Another example of the low esteem with which people view child care is found in an article in the *Wall Street Journal* about corporate involvement in day care. The writer says that one company, aware of the needs in its city for daytime infant care and overnight supervision for children of all ages, was going to donate cribs and other equipment to two family-day-care women. In return, the women agreed "to seek extra training, and refrain from smoking around their young charges."[11] All that is necessary are a few cribs, a little extra training, and a ban on smoking and the corporation has become socially active!

There are efforts to make the field of early-childhood education and child care more professional,[12] but there are impediments to doing so. In addition to the fact that it is women's work, it is also part of the historical development of teaching young children. That historic thread is one of low salary and even volunteerism. An outgrowth of the nineteenth-century European kindergarten movement, early-childhood education was brought to the United States by romantic, idealistic women. The work of Elizabeth Peabody on this subject is particularly significant. Peabody called working with the young a "mission," a "calling."[13] Sincere and dedicated women sacrificed monetary rewards for the spiritual, inner rewards they received from their work with the young. This tradition has meant that the teachers of young children have always essentially subsidized child care. But, dedication and sacrifice are no longer valued as occupational ideals. People entering the field will need other motivations.

History and tradition are not the only reasons for the low pay and low status of teachers in day care. Another reason is that our society does not, in fact, value its young. Parents and toy and book manufacturers push children into early achievement and accomplishment. Parents boast about early walkers, early talkers, and even early teeth. The child, who at two and a half has been trained to recognize the words STOP and EXIT and GAS when in the car, becomes, to some parents, the early reader. And so they buy products like infant flash cards and books like *How to Teach Your Baby to Read.*[14] "We didn't push her," they say. "She learned all by herself." It is interesting to contemplate the reasons for this desire to advance the years—for at the other end of the age scale, our society does not value the elderly. As we discharge more people from other institutions—prisons, mental hospitals, facilities for the retarded—we are creating more institutions for our young and for our old.

Despite the fact that society does not perceive it, there are, in fact, many necessary skills to be a good, even adequate, caretaker of young children. In *Who's Minding the Children?* Margaret Steinfels says: "As any visitor to a day care center soon realizes, it requires an enormously skilled, resourceful, sensitive person with great physical stamina and endurance to work effectively with young children. To be the supplementary parent of a three, four, or five year old is no easy task. We might idealize the mother or father of preschoolers as all sweetness and light, tiptoeing among the tulips, but they would probably last longer if they were six-foot, two-hundred-pound former decathalon champions."[15] The ideal day-care teacher would have eyes in the back of her head, at least six hands, quick reflexes, and a sense of humor. But, she'd better not have expensive taste if she is self-supporting.

Day-care teachers must be reliable, hard-working, cooperative, energetic, and well trained in education, in psychology, in sociology and in first aid. Whether they are called teachers or caregivers or assistants, they must be reliable about attendance. They know that children depend upon them. They know that it is almost impossible to find last-minute substitute teachers. They know that after they take a sick day, or a vacation, children are happy to see them back but will test them. Children, when in doubt about the reliability of an adult, often act out in aggressive or antisocial ways, to test the rules, to guarantee that things have returned to normal.

Jerome Kagan has pointed out that there are four primary motives for learning. One of these motives is to *resolve uncertainty.* "Mischievous behavior," he says, "is an attempt to obtain some information about the rules of living. . . . Children test limits with adults in order to find out what is permitted; they want to know the rules of each game, contest, or interaction so that they can more securely select future actions."[16] Mischievous behavior during and following a teacher's absence may be a learning experience for the child; but it can be harrowing for the substitute and for the returning teacher.

During the head teacher's absence, then, children behave a little wilder and test limits with the substitute. The substitute is probably ignorant of, and, in any case, unable to enforce, the ground rules of the group. The children have seen so many caregivers come and go that they wonder if their teacher actually will come back. They make educated, experiential deductions. Past experience has taught them that adults do leave often and do not come back. So when the head teacher returns, the children need reassurance that things have returned to normal. Reliability and stability are, thus, among the primary requisites for teachers of young children.

Teachers of young children must be hard workers. To run a good program, teachers must be well organized, with detailed plans for each day. But, because they work with children, they must be flexible, prepared for interruptions, changes, revisions of the schedule. They must be able to deal with parents in a professional, objective way while being warm and nurturing to the children. They must understand child development and adult development. They must be able to apply theories of development to the actual classroom. They must know about literature for children and nutrition for children, about fingerpaint and toilet training, about the use of space and about how to handle a woman whose husband has just abandoned her.

Day-care teachers must be healthy. There are, of course, state laws that require chest x-rays and physical examinations for adults who work with children. But day-care teachers in particular should have good resistance to viruses and infections, for the day-care center is a fertile place for the spread of illnesses. And, as indicated above, day-care teachers face additional problems with child behavior when they return after absences. Finally, as we have seen, some are not even paid for sick days.

Day-care teachers must have supervisory skills. They must, of course, be able to supervise and manage groups of children. In addition, they must be able to supervise assistants, volunteers, parent helpers. A day-care teacher might, in the course of several months, have a senior citizen and a student helper in her class. She must make them feel welcome and useful and teach them the rules of the group. Few, if any, people, young or old, appear at centers for young children and know how to act appropriately. They need training by modeling and by direction. The day-care teacher in her individual classroom, in addition to her many other responsibilities, has the responsibility for training.

Day-care teachers need interpersonal skills. They must work closely and intimately with other staff members. They must often share their space, equipment, and supplies with another shift of teachers. And, of course, they have to share their children with that other shift.

Because there is so little free time, teachers who share space can meet rarely to talk. Therefore, much of their communication is done in the presence of children or with notes to one another on paper or chalkboard. How do you tell a coworker, in front of eight small children, that she left the sand table a mess yesterday and should be more careful today? How does the afternoon teacher complain in the center log book that the morning teachers let the children get too overstimulated and loud and that they could never settle down that afternoon?

The day-care teacher also needs interpersonal skills to work with parents. Just as each child has individual needs, so too does each set of parents. Some need reassurance, some need instruction, some need limit setting, some need friends. Yet, the good day-care teacher cannot undermine her professional position by becoming a close friend. Dealings have to be warm and friendly, but professional boundaries must always be maintained.

The day-care teacher must be expert in protecting children from aggression. And she must be expert in teaching them how to control their own aggressive feelings. She must understand that some aggression is normal in any group of preschool children.

> Caregivers need to be . . . reasonably mature people who understand their own aggressive feelings and have them under control. . . . Constructive caregiving does not deny that hostile, angry feelings exist or try to stamp them out. It does limit children when they are acting out these angry feelings upon other children, protect them from one another, explain, comfort, and negotiate disagreements. It involves helping them gradually to learn, especially through demonstration and example, how to express their anger or hostile feelings verbally or in modulated rather than intense ways. It is impossible to create an environment for young children in which they learn to control and use their aggressive energy constructively unless there are a sufficient number of adults to guide them. . . . When there are not enough adults to guide young children away from physically aggressive encounters with one another and direct their energy into more constructive social and learning activities, the toddler's rooms become a nightmare. . . . Adults are harassed and overburdened; children are upset, angry, and unable to use the program productively.[17]

The day-care teacher must have stamina. Novelists and television script writers and cartoonists have portrayed and sometimes ridiculed the woman with the overwhelming burden of a large family. But, in reality, the mother with eight to ten children had to have them spaced so that at some point the older children could help with the younger children. If they did not help, at least their needs were different. And, of course, the burdens *were* overwhelming.

Group care for the young ignores biology by asking that some women take on the prolonged care and education of large numbers of children of the same age. "Well," some people say, "when they're not your own, you're not as emotionally involved." But day-care teachers are emotionally involved. They must convey a sense of love and trust to the children in their care. In addition, they must have seemingly endless energy.

Some researchers have recommended ratios of one adult to eight or ten children.[18] Those researchers should try to help that many children with their outdoor clothes for a week or so of a typical New England winter. They would soon learn that day care in a cold climate, with that kind of adult to child ratio, imitates the Keystone Kops comedies.

The teacher announces to the eight children that it is time to go outdoors. She reminds them all to go to the bathroom, then asks them to walk to their cubbies to get ready. Of the eight, three might run, three might walk, and two might continue to sit where they are. In any given group there is usually one supercompetent child who is dressed appropriately before half of the class has even found its cubbies. In most groups there is usually one child who *thinks* she is supercompetent and who puts on boots and jacket and then needs to be totally undressed to put on her snow pants. There is usually one child who becomes a lump of lead at dressing time. She just lies there waiting for an adult to do all the moving of stiff legs and arms. By the time the teacher has the fifth child ready to go outdoors, the first few are overheated and restless. They often resort to roughhousing among themselves or teasing the children still waiting to be helped. Finally, all the children are bundled up and the teacher and the group are walking through the door, the teacher putting on her jacket as she shepherds the children. Invariably, one child now will announce, "I have to go to the bathroom."

It is even more of a comedy watching younger children, at the toddler stage, get ready to go outdoors. Even with a one-to-three ratio, they present some interesting problems. Toddlers are very curious; they are anxious to try out all the miracles and mysteries of the world. The first toddler in the triad, all ready to go outdoors, cannot comprehend the necessity of sitting quietly and waiting for the others. She is a creature of the here and now. There is a whole world of exciting things to try. So she tries to go outside herself. The teacher has to rush to the door to scoop her up and, in the process, abandon the other two she was helping. One of those other children moves over to the puzzle rack and spills two puzzles. The teacher brings back the independent child, plunks her down firmly, and says in a calm voice, "Mandy, you need to wait until we are all ready." But the child only understands her own readiness. She seems to understand that she'd better not try to go out, so she looks at her jacket and wonders about the zipper. She has a human compulsion to experiment with and gain mastery over her environment, so she pulls down the zipper and, *mirabile dictu*, her jacket opens. That victory inspires her to try to get an arm out the sleeve. By the time her teacher has finished picking up the spilled puzzle pieces and has her other two charges ready—but before she has a chance to put on her own coat—the first toddler is totally undressed.

These behaviors are not exaggerated in any way. All teachers of the young have faced similar situations day after day and month after month. Their main hopes are for the growth and maturing of their children and the arrival of spring. They know that cognitively the behaviors they witness are age-appropriate. They understand that children are impelled by the human need to experiment and learn. But a teacher's understanding of the reasons, the whys for all of this, does little to ease her frustration or her fatigue.

After that monumental task, the teacher cannot take a coffee break with adults or sit quietly and read a book. Instead, she must supervise the next block of time on the schedule. If everything is going well that day, the next part of the program, although it is on a cold playground, might be fairly relaxed. The teacher might do as little as arbitrate about possession of the most popular tricycle on the playground. She might then push two children on swings or help a child who has just come back from vacation reenter the group. That scenario would describe a good day. On a bad day, after dealing with snowpants and boots, a teacher might have to comfort an injured child while chastising the child who caused the injury. A stray dog might be on the playground frightening one particular child. Or, a teacher might have to supervise extra children because of an emergency in another class.

The day-care teacher must have enough stamina to cope with the unexpected. She may work a six-hour shift and begin her day at the center at 7:30 in the morning, with the expectation that she'll be able to leave at 1:30 or 2:00. But if, at noon, the afternoon teachers call in sick and the director is unable to find substitutes, then the morning teacher and the director—or perhaps the cook—might have to stay until 6:00 P.M.

The day-care teacher must be expert in environmental design. She must design a space that is safe, attractive, stimulating but not overly so. If she is not so skilled, she will have to work with "the high level of sensory stimulation that is so common in child care. The bright lights, shrill sounds of the temper tantrum . . . tax most workers' sensory capacities."[19]

Day-care teachers must be thrifty. Their budgets for supplies are low, yet the hours when children need those supplies are long. They must make attractive, interesting activities out of what is euphemistically called scrounge materials or found materials or beautiful junk. They must save almost everything that might possibly have another use—from acorns to wrapping paper, from avocado seeds to yogurt containers. They must find the time to go to garage sales and church bazaars, rummage sales and flea markets. They must learn how to turn their own and other people's leavings into colorful, safe, child-appropriate equipment and materials.

In addition to the regular functions of caregiving, teaching, supervision of assistants, conferencing and counseling parents, teachers in the Whitebook study in San Francisco mentioned other added chores. These tasks included cleaning and cooking and working overtime for planning and staff meetings. Almost half the people in this study received no compensation for extra hours of work. Sixty percent spent up to ten dollars each month of their own money on supplies because of inadequate budgets.[20] They probably looked upon this as a wise investment, because if anything makes work with large groups of children intolerable, it is working without adequate, appropriate, and interesting supplies for children.

Another function many day-care workers must take on are those of advocacy. They must lobby not only for their own advancement but also for the rights of all children and families. They must serve as a pressure group at all levels of government, local, state, and federal, from matters as far ranging as candidate endorsements, lead-paint poisoning, and the mandatory use of seat belts.[21]

Day-care teachers must be mature. They spend the bulk of their working time nurturing others and they get little nurturing in return. Parents, boards of directors, and administrators may express appreciation for what the staff of a day-care center does, but that appreciation is rarely adequate. For parental appreciation is hardly ever based on a real understanding of the complexity of the work. "She likes children," parents will say. Or, in utmost respect, a mother might say, "I don't know how she does it. She must have the patience of a saint." Administrators often have a real understanding of the day-to-day life of a teacher in a day-care center, but only if they came up through the ranks and served as teachers themselves. Even so, they must struggle with balancing budgets, conforming to state codes for licensing, maintaining full enrollment, counseling staff and parents. They, themselves, although sometimes perceived as executives, often need nurturing, too.

The reality is that none of these people, teachers or directors, are saints. They need assurances that they are appreciated. They need positive feedback and praise. And they need tangible proof that they are valued. Yet, in a society that shows its value of people and things by the amounts of money they earn or cost, these workers, mostly women and mostly professionals, are not recognized as having any outstanding value. Therefore, day-care teachers must be sufficiently mature and self-confident to have a good sense of their own intrinsic value.

The most difficult task for the day-care teacher, and the one for which she gets the least credit, is the awesome responsibility she has for other people's lives. She is responsible for the health and safety of large numbers of children. No matter what the ratio of staff to child is, the head teacher feels that ultimate responsibility. She must be alert always to what is happening in all corners of her room or her playground. She can never slacken in her vigilance. In addition, she is responsible for the social and emotional development of each child in her care. When children develop symptoms of distress, like eneuresis or severe masturbation, she must always question why. She must consider the home situation; but she must also consider what she is doing. And so, sometimes she wonders if she is doing something wrong, if there is something she should be doing better or just plain differently. Further she has the responsibility for the cognitive growth of those children. She must strive at all times to keep each child intellectually satisfied, challenged but not frustrated. Finally, she has responsibility for each family. When she senses problems, she must determine whether they need to take up expensive consultation time. After making that decision, she often must determine how to deal with the parents so that they can all work together. She has this overwhelming responsibility and is then called a babysitter.

The major result of the low status and low pay of day-care teachers is staff burnout. Herbert Freudenberger in "Burn-out: Occupational Hazard of the Child Care Worker," has stated that "burnout includes such symptoms as cynicism and negativism and a tendency to be inflexible and almost rigid." Workers, he adds, become "bored with the work as well as with the kids."[22] Other authorities on burnout claim that it is characterized by both physical and emotional exhaustion and frequently leads to "a cynical and dehumanized perception" of the clients. Christina Maslach and Ayala Pines, in "The Burn-Out Syndrome in the Day Care Setting" add that "the person who dehumanizes others experiences less emotion, less empathy, and fewer personal feelings, and thus dehumanizes himself or herself as well."[23]

After a study of eighty-three day-care staff members, Maslach and Pines recommended higher staff-to-child ratios, shorter hours of actual direct work with children, a system of *time-outs* in which teachers could leave the classroom and do other tasks at the center, and more frequent staff meetings for mutual support. What is most interesting about these suggestions is that they are all very expensive. They involve more staff working fewer hours with children and that raises the costs considerably. The other interesting part of their proposal is the concept of time-outs. They suggest that these periods could be for "doing paperwork, preparing materials or food."[24] There it is, as plain as possible, back to the housekeeping and clerical roles of women. It was not suggested that these time-outs could be used for reading psychological and educational journals; writing case notes and developmental progress reports; consulting with clinicians and social workers; visiting other facilities for children; observing the other groups within the center; or any of the other possibilties of professional growth and interest. No. Time-outs are to be used for a break from the children but for stereotypically female tasks.

From all the studies of burnout, it seems clear that the problems teachers in day care face are situational rather than personal. Some teachers, of course, come with their own agendas, their own needs. But these personal needs are soon overshadowed by the realities of working with young children and balancing the demands with the rewards, the menial with the professional. "Child care practice is also marked with a seemingly inevitable role conflict . . . between client-care and custodial-managerial requirements"[25] According to Maslach and Pines, not enough research has been done into the stresses of child care work. Yet, to help staff members provide quality child care and teaching, it is necessary to understand both the stresses of the work and the ways each staff member copes with those stresses.[26]

If some day-care teachers suffer burnout, others, because of their low salary and low status, begin to see themselves as inferior or subordinate to the parents who use their facilities. One interesting result of this attitude is that some caretakers take on the characteristics of the subordinates that Jean Baker Miller speaks of in *Toward a New Psychology of Women*. Subordinates, she says, are those whose roles "typically involve providing services that no dominant group wants to perform for itself."[27] Because subordinates must concern themselves with basic survival, they do not consciously rebel against the dominant group. They accept the rules, which, as we have seen, in day care mean low pay, long hours, frequent burdening with inappropriate requests, low social status, little recognition for important learned and natural skills, and unusual personal risks to their own health. Parents, in turn, act like the classical dominant group by denying any inequality. "They can even believe that both they and the subordinate group share the same interests and, to some extent, a common experience."[28] Subordinates, according to Miller, do not rebel openly. But, they do have techniques for getting even. Day-care teachers, in order to get even for their low position, often become manipulative and exert control in a subtle, inadvertent manner. They learn how to look, how to act, and how to speak in clinical and educational jargon so that parents feel inadequate, even guilty. "We don't know why, but Alice has reverted to her sly, passive-aggressive behavior again," a teacher will say to a tired mother of a three-year-old child at the end of the day.

Subordinates have no power in our society and so they are driven to find devious ways of achieving some. They become "attuned to the dominants, able to predict their reactions of pleasure and displeasure."[29] They know more about the dominant group than the dominant group suspects and they use that knowledge to try to gain some subtle control. But, as Miller says, "tragic confusion arises because subordinates absorb a large part of the untruths created by the dominants."[30] And so, when day-care teachers see themselves considered and salaried as low-skilled workers, they begin to believe it themselves. All of their obvious skills, abilities, and responsibilities are denied even to themselves.

They find even more reinforcement in large statistical studies, also done by a dominant group. The National Day Care Study found that "neither education nor experience (of caregivers) could be shown to be a statistically significant determinant of classroom interactions or developmental test scores. Because both characteristics are related to cost but neither is related to any measure of the welfare or development of children, it seems inappropriate to incorporate either into future purchasing requirements."[31]

Dedicated and hard-working, sensitive and caring, day-care teachers finally see themselves as part of the bottom line of trade-offs. Their education and their experience have no statistical significance for quality, only for cost. Despite this kind of professional insult, day-care teachers must maintain self-respect, a positive self-image, and continue to be role models for the children they serve. It is a monumental task.

6 The Lives of Parents: Quantity versus Quality

A careful consideration of the realities of center-based day care indicates that the experience can be a difficult one for both children and staff. Although center-based care does have many advantages for its third major constituency—parents—it is problematic for them, too. And, in most cases, despite some relatively recent changes in the division of labor and assumption of responsibilities within families, the problems, the stresses, the difficulties confront mothers more often than fathers.

One of the advantages for parents of center-based care is that they can use licensed, controlled facilities. For some parents, this arrangement seems to guarantee adequate care, whereas there is no outside control or monitoring in most in-home or family-day-care situations. The semipublic nature of the day-care center makes it appear more reliable; the presence of numbers of adults is reassuring. Parents feel secure because even minimal licensing requirements include policies that presumably prevent neglect, abuse, or other forms of inappropriate treatment. These requirements include safety measures for both indoor and outdoor space; they include standards about staffing and about staff training; and they include regulations about program and curriculum. Center-based care, then, seems to be the most professional alternative for some families.

Parents also see the day-care center as a consistent place, open daily, without long vacations. In a fairly routine way, they can drop their children off in the morning and pick them up in the late afternoon or evening. For busy working parents, the center option can mean a much more satisfying arrangement than a complex patchwork of various caretakers, locations, and transportation arrangements. There might still be a patchwork of caretakers, but the juggling will be handled by the day-care-center administration rather than by the parents themselves. In addition, the parent is less likely to see the large numbers of teachers and assistants that the child sees. Rather, the parent sees the limited staff who are present early and late in the day. Above all, many arrangements for child care are complicated and fragile. One interruption in the structure often sends the whole thing tumbling. If children are in one setting for forty-five or fifty hours a week, there are fewer chances for this kind of fragility.

If there are major separation problems for a child in center-based care, the acting out usually subsides after an initial adjustment period. Besides, many children have separation difficulties in other forms of care as well as in center care. Once parents have decided that supplemental care is required, they must cope with the separation issue whether it is at a center, in a family-day-care home, in the home of a friend or relative, or even if it is in-home care. Many parents feel more confidence in the professional handling of separation difficulties at a day-care center than they feel in other caregivers.

Some parents are reassured about day-care centers by people they consider experts: the researchers and early-childhood educators who help make up the day-care lobby. Although parents may see day-care centers as the best answer for their own needs, they often see it as the best answer for their children's needs, too. They are comforted by the knowledge that so many child-development professionals endorse and even recommend center-based care. Many parents are not aware of any of the ambivalences and caveats of some experts. Perhaps because they have neither the time nor the energy, many day-care parents do not concern themselves about issues like leashes, cagelike cribs, or health risks. And, parents are reassured when day-care professionals talk in jargon and claim educational and social gains for children raised in groups.

One example of that research jargon can be drawn from a study of infant day care. "Infants in day care engaged in more reciprocal and stimulating interaction with their caregivers than their counterparts at home. Infants in day care exhibited more positive affect throughout the day than did toddlers at home, and played at a higher developmental level with toys."[1] It is no wonder that parents feel reassured about the day-care experience for young children. It is no wonder that they overlook many of the negative aspects of institutionalization, especially if they feel that they are helping their child get "reciprocal and stimulating interactions." Because they might wish to hasten their child's development and consequent independence, they might be impressed with the idea of infants playing at higher developmental levels.

For some parents, then, center-based care appears to be the best option. But just as there are problems for the other two major day-care constituencies, there are also problems for parents; for center-based care is not always what parents would choose if in fact they had other options. Suzanne Woolsey in "Pied Piper Politics and the Child Care Debate" refers to three studies that indicate that center-based care is not the option of first choice. She cites a 1968 study that found that parents were most satisfied with at-home arrangements. She also describes a 1970 survey by the Westinghouse Corporation that found that most people across all income groups would choose informal care either in the child's home or in the neighborhood. In this survey, parents expressed the following preferences for types of care, in this order: proximity to home, costs, hours of operation, care for sick children, and program.[2]

Finally, Woolsey discusses a 1975 Department of Health, Education, and Welfare Survey in which 63 percent of those families sampled preferred to have their children taken care of by relatives. Fifty-three percent expressed a preference for care in their own homes. The most satisfactory care for nearly everyone was reported to be care by relatives either in their homes or in the children's homes.[3]

Perhaps one primary reason for the preference for care by a relative is that it often solves the cost issue. Even though center-based care is less expensive than many other forms of care, it does consume a large percentage of family income. For young families, cost, of course, must be a major consideration. In fact, many families are able to arrange for care at no cost. In Kamerman's study of two-hundred working mothers with preschool children, 27 percent paid nothing for their child care.[4] In another study of working mothers, 49 percent relied mainly on relatives and paid nothing for day care.[5] And, of the twenty-five families that Laura Lein studied in the Working Family Project, eleven did not pay for their child care.[6]

However, cost may not be the only reason for the preference of care by relatives. Parents want their children raised with their own values, in their own style. For instance, Lein found that working families considered outside influences one of the major threats to family life.[7] Certainly, parents must feel that members of the immediate or extended family are the most likely to agree with their values and transmit them to the next generation.

Still another possible reason for the preference of care by a relative is because it offers a great deal of flexibility and resilience. These attributes, flexibility and resiliency, are necessary to accommodate for emergencies. All families, and especially all young working families, have emergencies. There are times when a child is ill; there are other times when parents are ill and cannot either care for the child or transport her to a caretaker; there are times when professional demands require parents to work overtime or on weekends, or to go out of town at the last minute. Most day-care centers are not designed to offer service in such emergencies. They are not equipped to handle sick children; they are not staffed for evenings or overnights or weekends. Therefore, even with the best center arrangements, most parents must have back-up support services for emergencies and for some overnight care. From a child-centered point of view, these supports should be people familiar to the child rather than strangers. If parents do not have adequate back-up support services for last-minute crises, then they must have flexibility in their own jobs so that they themselves can be available. Unfortunately, if they have neither back-up supports nor job flexibility, they run the risk of damaging their own careers.

A large part of our society has not yet acknowledged that when young children are growing up, there are always last-minute emergencies. A large part of our society seems to forget that the working parent in the marketplace often must respond to family commitments as a priority over professional commitments. Thus, when parents face the conflicting demands of work and of children, they are often in a no-win situation. The needs and demands of one or the other must be neglected or overlooked. One result is that those who care for the children in day-care centers often resent the fact that physically ill children are still brought to the center. Or, they disapprove of hasty, last-minute arrangements that leave a child bewildered and confused. On the other hand, however, employers do not condone employee absences because of sick-child care. And, if employers observe that parents are not cooperative or flexible about travel or about working extra hours or weekends, their observations may impede promotions. Thus, one study of families found that people from a variety of groups and life styles agree that "people who expect to get ahead in their careers or jobs have to expect to spend less time with their families."[8]

Many of the issues of day-care parents, then, are inherent in the very nature of the working-parent situation. There are so many problems, and the day-care center cannot possibly deal with all of them. Unfortunately, the person who customarily deals with all of those problems is the mother. Even in the most supportive, two-parent families, the female, the wife, the mother, seems to get the overwhelming responsibility for managing the daily lives of the family, as well as the emergencies.

In the decade from 1970 to 1980, there were more than four thousand entries related to parent-child relationships in the publication *Psychological Abstracts*.[9] Some of that research implies that fathers' roles are changing and that they are participating more fully in the care and raising of their children. Other studies indicate that although there are slight statistical increases in father participation, the major responsibility for maintaining the home and for caring for the young falls on the mother. If the mother also happens to work outside the home, she spends less time in the performance of her other responsibilities than the at-home mother. But, the differences do not balance; that is, the working mother must put in more total or combined hours to meet all of her responsibilities. She does so, according to one study, with less sleep.[10]

Whatever changes are taking place are quite minimal and hesitant. As Joseph Pleck has found, men with working wives are now participating more in family activities than are men whose wives do not work.[11] In the mid-1960s Pleck conducted a study that showed that men spent approximately 11.2 hours per week in family work. Housewives spent 53.2 hours per week in such work; working women spent 28.1 hours at it. In a later study in the mid-1970s, Pleck found that husbands of working wives spent 1.8 more hours in housework and 2.7 more hours in child care than did husbands of nonworking wives.[12] Another indication of this slight increase in male participation in family work and child care is found in the General

Mills study, *Families at Work*. Parents in about one-third of the households with children at home claim that mothers and fathers share the care equally.[13] Finally, one reviewer of the literature of the last ten years has said that "fathers are more nurturant than many would have believed a decade ago."[14]

Changes such as these, however, are hardly large enough to generate much optimism about the role of men in the family. In fact, Pleck cites other studies in which only a small percentage of those sampled felt that men should participate more in housework and child care than they now do. In a number of studies, there is no consensus at all that men should spend more time at family work.[15]

In *Sooner or Later*, a study of eighty-six couples, Daniels and Weingarten found that women remain responsible for raising children in our society. They say that "so long as women bear the sole, or even primary responsibility for the care of preschool children . . . they are likely to experience conflict and overload."[16] Elsewhere, they say that "in the short-run . . . the price of holding down two demanding occupations, one at home and the other away, is high: constant fatigue and overloaded circuits."[17] "All of the simultaneous double-duty mothers experienced the 'something has to give' feeling. In no other situation was so much conflict so consistently reported."[18]

In a description of another study, the author states that "while not minimizing the strain on the father in the dual-worker families, the Working Family Project saw the mother as subject to more pressures. The toll women paid in trying to assume new responsibilities along with the old was a sense of being rushed constantly, under pressure, never able to relax or consider a job properly finished."[19]

And, another writer says that "the conflicts between work and family roles are seldom resolved, rather they are 'juggled' in a time-budgeting process that is often unsatisfactory. Because of the traditional division of labor within the family it is the woman who is seen as principally responsible for domestic chores, including child care. The strain of overload is most often felt, therefore, by the mother who works."[20]

Professional status does not seem to make a large difference in this pattern. In a sample of almost two hundred physicians, women doctors worked 90 percent as much as their male counterparts. But 76 percent of the women did all of the shopping, cooking, child care, and management of money for the household. Almost none of the men sampled had any household responsibilities except for money management. More women than men claimed that they had changed their career plans because of either a relationship or because of child-related responsibilities. Despite the added commitment to responsibilities for home and children by the women, 54 percent felt that there were too many demands on their energy; 60 percent of the men felt that way.[21] Thus, although women have more demands placed on them, they complain about them less!

When asked about the tenure issue at Harvard University, President Derek Bok said, "We don't necessarily understand all the problems and obstacles and complexities in women getting tenure, but one of them may be that some women have greater burdens and responsibilities resulting from family obligations—regardless of whether they should or not—than men of the same age with whom they compete."[22]

Women in other professions, too, encounter similar experiences. In a study of French executives, a sociologist found data that sounds applicable to what is now happening in the United States. As reported in the *American Bar Association Journal*, the French study found that "married men do best and married women worst."[23] According to the study, wives support their husbands' careers but do not take their own careers seriously. Married women tend to leave work to do their domestic chores. Married men, however, work overtime to promote their professional lives. Thus, even without children, women who have responsibilities to both homes and careers are stretched thin and suffer for it.

There are people who look upon the problems as soluble if there is adequate money. In an article in the *New York Times*, one expert on the issue of working mothers said that mothers need adequate household help as well as income to support that help. In addition, they need health, energy, and strong support systems. All of the women interviewed for the article agreed that it was essential to have someone else totally responsible for running the household. And, they reported that they curtailed their social lives, spent their weekends with their families, got along on less sleep, and did professional paperwork at night. In this way these particular women found quality time for their children.[24]

Over a year later, the *New York Times* dealt with the same issue in a cover story in its Sunday magazine. Called "Careers and the Lure of Motherhood," the article mentions the "extra-ordinary psychological overload," the "juggling" women must do to manage careers, marriages, and children. The author says that many women regret that they cannot really enjoy either their children or their careers. And, many find that their Saturdays are miserable; they are a "two-career purgatory," with too little time to do all of the necessary family and household tasks, the food shopping, and the laundry. It is another irony of day care that weekends are when parents are told they can have quality time with their children. A two-career Saturday purgatory hardly qualifies as quality. The author also says that many working mothers are finding that by the time they pay for all of the necessary supports, their net gain is hardly worth the price they are paying in stress and in being separated from their child. The article cites a clinical psychologist who says that these couples have "an anhedonic quality." That is, they seem to have a sense of "joylessness," of "powerlessness," and "an inability to experience pure pleasure."[25]

On the same day as the *New York Times* article appeared, Art Buchwald, the humorist, published a column called "The woman behind the liberated woman." Buchwald points out, with as much pathos as humor, that the successful career woman needs someone to do the menial tasks for her. The fictional narrator of the piece notices, with irony, that a woman, to be free, needs to find a "slave" as a replacement at home. The narrator then asks the fictional "liberated woman" what she does when her household help is sick. She admits that she stays home. And, when she does, all the people in her law firm say, "We knew this would happen if we hired a *woman* lawyer."[26]

Thus, scholars and journalists and humorists are all concerned with the difficulties of being a working mother. And, whether the subject is dealt with statistically or in interviews or as satire, it is clear that society is doing little to help women with these issues. The quality of life of women, like that of children, is not a first, not a central priority in our society.

It seems that women have been sold a bill of goods. Compete with men, take on men's responsibilities, they have been told. Act the way they act, do what they do, and you will be equally rewarded. But, at the same time, maintain the old customs. Bear the children and rear the children. Do the cooking and do the laundry. And, do all of this without any role models, any help from a previous generation. Be competent and capable, ambitious and androgynous, and simultaneously, have the children and run the households. When emergencies arise, though, be like a man and do not let them interfere with your career or your career will suffer. While you are doing all this, give your children quality time.

The subject of quality time is another irony in the day-care experience. Researchers and licensors, in their search for scientific facts and bases for policy, speak in terms of *quantity*. They look for measurable variables that they can calculate in statistically valid ways. They reduce a dynamic, organic, living process to raw numbers. In doing so, they often neglect some of the realities of what they are analyzing. They call living, breathing children FTEs, for Full-time Equivalents. They analyze adult-child ratios on the basis of ADA, or Average Daily Attendance. They translate their findings into aggregates for cost-benefit purposes. Day-care advocates then seize upon these numbers and advertise them to the public to reassure them that day care is a proven and safe way to grow up. They determine the quality of a day-care center by quantitative means.

But then, these same advocates, when asked about parent-child relationships and surrogate or supplemental care, say, "Oh, it's not the quantity of time you spend with your child, it's the quality." If that time is made up of positive, pleasant, productive interactions, then it is quality. It is, some professionals assert, far more of a quality experience than being with an unhappy, uninterested, or unresponsive parent for long hours. Clearly, those parents who look upon their weekends as purgatory are not giving much quality time to their children. And, it is only logical that there is not much quality in the parents' lives.

The two-parent working family may gain some quality for their lives in terms of the increase in income. But, of course, the expenses of child care and other support services often outweigh the gains made in gross salary. And, if parents are always juggling, if they are experiencing overloads, both psychological and physical, if they are always feeling rushed, pressured, conflicted, guilty, fatigued, then time spent with their children cannot be quality time—either for the parents or for the children.

Those who are concerned with the lives of children must wonder what kinds of adults children are learning from. Their female models in many day-care centers are overworked and underpaid; their own parents, but especially their mothers, are also overworked and stretched thin. Children, then, may be learning a mode of behavior, especially of female behavior, that is always brittle; that is always on a short fuse; that is tired, overworked, harassed. It is too early to know what effects such role models and prototypes will have on the young. One possible result is that a new generation will have more disdain for women than preceding generations had. The work of the last decade to erase old stereotypes may in fact create new ones. In terms of the quality of the life experience, women and children are, once again, not first, not primary, not even equal. And the day-care center, already burdened with many responsibilities, cannot possibly assume the additional responsibility for the quality of life for working mothers. It cannot solve the myriad of problems facing the working family with preschool children.

7 Budgets and Bottom Lines

The conflicts of the day-care constituencies are nowhere more evident than they are in the area of costs. Most parents who use day-care centers for child care cannot afford to spend large amounts of money to pay for that care. In fact, many choose center-based care because it is less expensive than in-home care with a paid sitter or housekeeper. It is also less expensive than some forms of small group, out-of-the-home care. Fees may be lower than these other forms of care, but those fees must support day-care staff and must provide for all of the various necessities of the day-care center.

An examination of the figures leads to a conclusion common about day care. It is a no-win situation. Parents must spend large percentages of their earnings. These expenditures are transformed into minimal, sometimes exploitative, wages for teachers. The teachers often work under stressful conditions and the children are frequently in overcrowded, dehumanizing facilities. Parents who complain of the high costs of child care should examine carefully the budgets of the centers they use. In a world of trade-offs, they should consider exactly what they are buying for their children.

Each child, each family, and each day-care service is different and has different needs; so too is each day-care-center budget different from all others. Some budgets are based on comprehensive costs and services and include rent, transportation, food services, and health services. Other budgets are for centers in donated spaces at work sites, churches, or universities, and, therefore, do not necessarily have occupancy costs or transportation costs. Still other budgets are at centers with many volunteers and/or student teachers so that their salary costs might be lessened. Yet, if those centers have a major responsibility for teacher training, their own teachers might command larger salaries based on education, experience, and skills. Although there is a range of salaries and fringe benefits for day-care workers, their salaries never match those of public-school teachers. Low as the day-care salaries are, they can consume up to 90 percent of some center budgets. Some centers spend under 50 percent of their budgets on salaries, and one proprietary profit-making center spends only 25 percent of its total budget on salaries.[1]

Some centers charge for the hours that children attend, while others charge each family for the entire time the center is open. Some charge by the hour, some by the time block. At some centers, full time means seven in the morning to six at night, while at others, it means nine to three. Some centers charge by the week, others by the month. Some centers are operated for profit, some are nonprofit but self-supporting, and others are nonprofit but subsidized. Therefore, it is virtually impossible to arrive at a recommended cost for day care. It is also virtually impossible to talk of percentages.

A 1976 study of day care analyzed budgets according to a functional breakdown of costs. It found that 49 percent was for care and teaching; 18 percent for administration; 12 percent for nutrition; 9 percent for occupancy; 5 percent for social services; 3 percent for training; 3 percent for transportation; and 1 percent for health.[2]

A center that does not provide either transportation or food would have another 15 percent to work with. This percentage could take the form of lower fees, more expenditures for care and teaching, or, in a for-profit day-care center, part or all of that sum could be returned to its investors or owners. Although each day-care center is different in its budgetary needs and policies, all centers share the task of managing on a severely restricted budget. Of course, no service in the economy, not even a service for children, can or should operate on an unrestricted budget. But in day care, budget restrictions have serious program implications. Budget restrictions have a heavy impact on the day-care-center environment. They limit the total amount of square footage per child and cause the imaginative, but at times disturbing, multiple use of space. In fact, it is possible that some of the disease transmission in day-care centers is caused by the multiple purposes of their space. Budget restrictions in this area also affect the cleanliness of the space. More money spent on maintenance and custodial services generates a cleaner environment. These restrictions also influence the location and age of the space used. New buildings, designed specifically for young children and located in high-rent neighborhoods, unless financially subsidized, cost more than space in run-down, underoccupied buildings. Space costs are, then, one of the major reasons that so many centers are located in basements of churches or of academic buildings.

Budget restrictions affect the quantity and quality of outdoor space. Thus, there is a range of playground space from spacious, wooded areas on college campuses to bare asphalt yards bordering railroad tracks. Once there was even the suggestion to locate a day-care center in a space adjacent to an outdoor rifle-shooting range. The range was used for SWAT (special weapons and tactics) team practices that involved mock raids, shrieking sirens, and even fire-arms practice from the roof of the very building proposed as a day-care facility. Fortunately, a local early-childhood-development association vetoed the proposed location.[3]

Budget restrictions influence the selection of equipment and supplies. There are licensed centers that are forced to make do with few of the essentials for a sound program. Puzzles have missing pieces, books have missing pages, dolls have missing limbs. Teachers have arrived at new jobs to find no paper, no crayons, no paints. "They are on order," one director of a national franchise center told her staff. But if the teachers at that center really wanted to provide some constructive calm during the day, they had to spend their own money for these essentials. The Whitebook study of day-care staffs found that teachers did, indeed, spend their own money for supplies.[4]

Budget restrictions have an important impact on the nutrition and health standards of a center. Some centers dilute fruit juice with water to save money. One center has the children, ages two-and-a-half to five, rinse out their paper cups for reuse. At that particular center, a licensed one, children sit on the floor for their snack. Their crackers, one per child, are put down on the bare floor without even a paper napkin underneath. "They're so much happier sitting on the floor than they would be at a table," said the owner of that for-profit day-care center.

Perhaps the largest impact of the budget restriction is on staff. These restrictions affect the quality, the contentment, the job longevity, the numbers, and the leadership of the staff—with a consequent impact on the children at the center. Despite all these program implications and shortages of funds for the operation of day-care centers, the costs to parents do seem substantial and, to some people, exorbitant. National studies have shown that families spend 10 percent of their gross income on day care. It is estimated to be the fourth largest budget item after housing, food, and taxes.[5] In the summer of 1982, in a suburban community outside of Boston, Massachusetts, advertised fees for day-care centers had a large range. There were ads for $50.00 per week for an 8:00 A.M. to 6:00 P.M. day; for $75.00 per week in a 6:30 A.M. to 6:00 P.M. day; and for $95.00 per week in a 7:30 A.M. to 6:00 P.M. day. In that same summer of 1982, a resident of Manhattan claimed that she was spending $32.75 per day for center-based care.[6] And later, in the fall of 1982, one Boston area center was charging $600 per month, or $150 per week for infant day care.[7]

Comparisons of these figures are not indicative of the quality of care at any of these facilities, because there is no way of knowing from their ads how these fees are spent. If, for instance, the fifty dollar per-week fee is for a center that has space, administrative costs, and health services donated by a local corporation, it might be of higher quality than the center charging ninety-five dollars per week. However, if it is operating as a for-profit center, without any in-kind subsidy, one can be fairly certain that it will be of inferior quality compared to the more expensive site; for according to the National Day Care Study, for-profits spend 30 percent less on child care than nonprofit centers.[8]

Costs for infants and toddlers are generally higher than for preschoolers because younger children require more staff per number of children. Therefore, the center that charges $75 per week for its four year olds might charge

$90 per week for toddlers and $120 per week for infants. The figures in these examples are higher than many quoted national averages. For instance, one analyst states that the average cost for care in a center is $2,000 per year, or approximately $40 per week.[9] And the July 1982 issue of *Working Mother* refers to a number of national day-care chains that charge between $45 and $70 a week for the care of infants. The president of a national chain, one with ninety centers, was quoted as saying, "We don't make any money at all on infant care."[10]

Tax deductions do provide some help to parents. There is a tax credit of 30 percent of work-related expenses for adjusted gross incomes of $10,000 or less. That percentage is reduced by one point for each $2,000 of adjusted gross income over $10,000, ending at 20 percent for incomes above $28,000. In other words, the smaller the income, the larger the percentage of tax credit. The maximum amount of work-related expense is $2,400 for one child and $4,800 for two or more. Thus, the family with the minimum income and the greatest allowable work-related expense could conceivably get a tax credit of $720 for one child and $1,440 for two or more. However, it seems unlikely that a family with an adjusted gross income of $10,000 could afford such large out-of-pocket child-care expenditures. Those families at the higher end of the income scale would receive a lower percentage of work-related child-care expenses to credit. They could claim 20 percent of $2,400, or $480 for one child; and 20 percent of $4,800, or $960 for two or more children.[11] But even with these deductions, the strains on the family, as well as the financial limitations on day-care budgets, are severe.

If there is any proof of the attitude of society toward its young, perhaps the most poignant is a comparison of day-care tuition figures with those of the Northampton (Mass.) State Hospital. The hospital is a facility for mentally ill patients without medical insurance, who have been diagnosed as posing a threat to themselves or to others. According to the *Boston Globe*, Northampton Hospital can spend $50,000 per patient per year. This expenditure is possible because Northampton's total budget has remained the same, although its patient population has declined considerably. Despite that expenditure, patients receive an average of four hours of direct therapy per week. They spend the bulk of their time pacing the wards, watching television, and sleeping. The Northampton sum does not seem outrageous compared to a private mental hospital outside of Boston that charges $100,000 a year per patient for room, board, and nursing care, exclusive of psychiatric care.[12]

Another poignant comparison is between day-care-center costs and prisons. It is estimated that it costs between $15,000 and $20,000 per year to keep and guard prison inmates.[13]

There is yet another group in our society whom we do not appear to cherish, yet on whom we spend more money than we do on our children.

They are the elderly. In the financial report of a nursing-home facility for the elderly in Boston for the year 1981, figures are given for total days of care given and for total expenditures. Simple division gives the figure of fifty-eight dollars per day as the cost for being at that center.[14]

It may seem spurious to compare costs for child day care and costs for residential centers for the mentally ill or for prisoners or for the elderly. Yet, the contrasts in per-person expenditures should inspire some new explorations. The contrasts may indicate that the amounts we designate as appropriate for spending on children, are, in fact, inadequate. And, if they are grossly inadequate, then parents and policymakers should begin to question their bottom-line, cost-benefit priorities. A rearrangement of priorities might constitute more far-sighted economics as well as more humane childhoods for the young.

8 The Day-Care Cloaca

Some physicians have referred to day-care centers as the cloacas of our society. In zoology, a *cloaca* is the common chamber into which the intestinal, urinary, and generative canals discharge in birds, reptiles, amphibians, and many fishes. The main drain or sewer under the city of Rome was, and still is, known as the Cloaca Maxima. Hence, the term *cloaca* has come to mean a general repository of filth and rubbish, of germs and bugs, of dirt and disease, as well as the products of infection and ingestion.

The cloaca label reflects one of the ironies of day care. As a humane institution, as an outgrowth of the kindergarten and early-childhood movements, day-care centers should contribute to the health of children. And in an ideal world, they would. They would ensure physical examinations before enrollment for all children; they would guarantee that all of their enrolled children had up-to-date, appropriate immunizations; they would be alert to warning signs of illnesses or handicaps; they would provide education and consultation to parents about nutrition, physical development, hygiene, and dental care; they would be able to provide nurturing, comfortable care for emergency illnesses.

An examination of centers in the real world, however, indicates that perhaps the word *cloaca* is justified for some centers. And, these centers are not necessarily located in slums or areas of heavy poverty. They are as varied as day-care centers come; they are both urban and suburban; they serve private clients and clients whose tuitions are federally funded; they are subsidized centers and nonsubsidized centers; they are operated for profit and not-for-profit.

In this real world of the 1980s young parents are often separated from their extended families and live rather isolated lives in neighborhoods where all of the adults are off doing something else. They are faced with dilemmas when their children become ill. Their jobs are important and their employers are annoyed if they stay home to care for a sick child. Because there are no emergency services or grandmothers around, some parents tend to minimize illnesses and send sick children to day care. In the early morning household rush, it is easy for parents—consciously or unconsciously—to ignore the beginnings of an illness.

In addition, parents have a positive, trusting attitude toward their centers and about the kinds of care their children will receive. A staff's commitment to good physical care helps ease parents' anxieties about their long separations.[1] Parents tend to perceive the center as a capable and available extended family. They see nothing wrong in bringing a symptomatic child who might be better off at home.

Current medical practices have not helped the situation. Twenty-five years ago, children with high fevers and symptoms of viral or bacterial infections would have been seen in house calls. Now, they are brought to pediatric offices and health-maintenance organizations for examinations. Ideas about contagion and about protection from exposure to other germs have become old-fashioned.

Day-care-center staff members often find it impossible to enforce rules about sick children remaining at the center. First of all, many children are delivered to the day-care center before their own head teacher, or primary caretaker, has arrived. In the early morning confusion, children are often still sleepy and cranky when separating from their parents. It can be difficult for the staff member on duty to make a rational, informed decision as to whether or not the child belongs at the center. In addition, if the staff member does not know the child or the parents well enough, she might be reluctant to insist that parents take a sickly looking child home for the day. Finally, the staff is sensitive to all the difficulties of the day for parents, both before and after they deliver the child to the center; therefore, the staff tends to hope that if the parents brought the child, then the child must be in good health.

The situation becomes even more complex when a child develops symptoms during the course of the day. Day-care teachers are aware of the problems facing the working parent. They are reluctant to interrupt the parental working day unless they are sure that the child needs to be taken home. They also know that sometimes, even if they reach a parent, that parent might be unable to pick up the child in a reasonable amount of time. Space and staff limitations add complexity, because teachers cannot always isolate the sick child or even take the time to phone the parents.

Efforts by the staff to make parents more sensitive to the health problems of children often have negative repercussions. Some parents become defensive. Parental defensiveness led to the staff of one center coining the phrase *lilacs and raisins* as its code words for sick children. That particular center was located on a college campus and served the children of professional parents. It had just set new restrictions on bringing sick children to the center because several viruses had been rampant among children and staff. One day a mother brought her child to the center and said that Alice might have diarrhea that day. The teachers should not be concerned; it was only because the child had eaten too many raisins for breakfast. The next child brought to that same classroom was sneezing and had a runny nose. "It's not a cold and it's not contagious," said her father. "It's an allergy to lilacs."

Just as some parents become defensive about center-staff efforts to raise their awareness of health issues, other parents develop guilt and consequent anger at the child and at the center. It is unlikely that any day-care teacher consciously wants to foster guilt in the parents she serves. She knows that that outcome will only have damaging effects on the child, on the parents, and eventually on her whole program. It is a difficult challenge for even the most skillful teacher or administrator to help parents deal appropriately with the issues of sickness and health. Of course, it is not just parents who are to blame for the cloaca syndrome. Teachers, too, in the pressure of their jobs, are sometimes careless about maintaining a healthful, sanitary environment.

Another important cause of the health problem is inherent in child growth and development. Young children learn with their senses. To understand an object, they must touch it; they must smell it; they must taste it. Therefore, toys, like fingers and thumbs, are often licked, tasted, sucked. Adults will scold, "Oh, Chrissie, take that out of your mouth!" But the child is behaving in an age-appropriate way; she is trying to make sense of her world.

Food, its preparation and serving, presents another problem, for day-care centers serve midmorning and midafternoon snacks in addition to lunch; and some must serve breakfast. Whether the food is prepared at the center or is brought from home by the children, it is often eaten under less than ideal conditions. It frequently is served on the same tables that are used for art and other activities. Staff members who assist children with toileting and diapering may not do the actual cooking or preparing but often must help in the distribution, serving, and feeding of meals and snacks. Because of time pressures, these staff members cannot always supervise hand-washing of the children to make sure that they have done a satisfactory job before eating. And, it is not unusual to see a child reach a hand inside her pants for a quick scratch before sitting down to eat.

Young children are developing social skills. Part of their social interaction involves curiosity and interest about their friends' possessions. Satisfying curiosity often involves tasting those possessions. Another part of the social interaction of children involves sharing. Children exchange food and pacifiers and all kinds of potential germ carriers. Young children have not yet learned etiquette or hygiene. It may seem gross to adults, but children must satisfy their interest in their immediate world. And so, they pick their noses and then taste what they have found. They use sleeves and arms instead of tissues to wipe their noses, if in fact they wipe them. They rarely cover their mouths during sneezes or coughs. They may sprinkle a few drops of water on their hands after toileting and consider the job well done. Or, they may wash and rinse and wring their hands with soap and water for ten minutes and want to continue for ten minutes longer.

All of this behavior is age-appropriate for young children. Parents and teachers must try to help children learn hygienic habits; but it takes patience, understanding, cognitive growth, and, mostly, time. Of course, no healthy child should grow up in an absolutely sterile, germ-free environment; but, the spread of germs in day-care centers is encouraged by the very nature of the young child.

Toddlers in the midst of being trained and those just newly trained present other kinds of problems. In a day-care center several children often share the same potty. As part of their pride, their sense of accomplishment, their drive to master their environment, toddlers often want to empty and rinse the potty bowl themselves. Once again, it is important to visualize how much supervision the average classroom teacher or assistant can give to this learning experience. And so, in the interests of growth and development, sacrifices are made about sanitation.

Perhaps the most important cause of unsanitary conditions is the closed environment of the day-care center. If it has infants and toddlers, then teachers must deal with diapers as well as the rashes and the smells and the germs that accompany diapers. Even in these modern times of disposable diapers, soiled ones must remain in diaper pails or plastic trash bags until custodial help arrives. A room that accommodates four infants or nine toddlers will also accommodate an equal number—or more—of diapers in its pail in just one morning. If custodial help does not arrive until the afternoon, and if the teachers themselves cannot empty the pail or discard the bag, then, of course, larger quantities of soiled diapers accumulate.

A social worker had to visit the day-care center of a client's child and complained because it smelled of disinfectant. She soon realized, however, that unless the rooms smelled of disinfectant, they would smell of human waste. Even those centers that do not enroll infants or toddlers, that insist on children being toilet trained before admission, have problems. Children with no obvious symptoms can be carriers of germs and infections. The day-care center is generally warm and always occupied with large numbers of children who eat, play, and sleep in the same room. The room itself becomes an incubator for various germs and viruses. Good centers also want children to learn about nature, to become caring and nurturant, and so they often have pets. The same room that is used for playing, eating, and sleeping often has in it a gerbil or a family of gerbils, a rabbit, or a guinea pig or two. Some centers have them all. Already burdened staff then have animals to feed and cages to clean. Even the most conscientious teacher will have some occasions when, for the sake of duties of higher priority or because of fatigue, she will neglect some part of that responsibility.

Unfortunately, the health issue seems to receive more attention in medical journals than it does in specific day-care literature. A random look at the treatment of health in a small but diverse selection of books on day care is quite revealing. Allison Clarke-Stewart, in *Daycare*, says "Children in day care centers get more flu, rashes, colds, and coughs than children at home." But, she adds, "A child's runny nose may be a price mothers are willing to pay . . . especially if most of the wiping of that nose is done by the day care staff."[2] This kind of flippancy is pertinent not just to health issues in day care but also to issues of staff self-concept and morale. It is no wonder that day-care teachers have classic symptoms of burnout if this is how their role is perceived.

In *Who's Minding the Children?* Steinfels points out that good health habits and health supervision were important aspects of early day nurseries. One example she uses of good health habits is the fact that some day-care centers insist that children brush their teeth after snacks and meals.[3] She does not describe, however, the kind of supervision, or lack of it, given to the actual brushing of the teeth or to the care and storage of the toothbrushes. Curious, social children are likely to experiment, to see if John's pink toothbrush feels the same as Anne's green one does. It would be most useful—and amusing—to observe a caregiver in a setting with a one-to-ten ratio of adults to children teach and enforce healthy, sanitary, after-snack and after-meal toothbrushing practices with three year olds!

In *The Challenge of Daycare*, the authors talk briefly of the physical environment, but they make no mention of the epidemics that can occur in settings for young children. In their recommendations about consultants, they refer to one for "health, including health-care practices, health education, nutrition, and first aid."[4] The realities of day care are, however, that few day-care centers have funds budgeted for such consultants or for the expense of staff time that such work would require. In *Who Cares for the Baby?* Beatrice Glickman and Nesha Springer state that "a good center will probably have a sick bay to care for mildly ill children." But they also speak of "bad" centers that meet government regulations, but whose "children seem subject to interminable cases of sniffles and diaper rash."[5]

That this is the case is not surprising, especially when one examines some examples of teacher-training literature. Most of the texts for future workers in early-childhood education emphasize the importance of first aid and of the preventative aspect of immunizations and regular checkups. Teacher-training books deal with dental care and nutrition education; they stress, and with good reason, all the caveats about safety both indoors and out. But, some of the literature seems quite casual about health. Carol Seefeldt, in *A Curriculum for Child Care Centers*, talks about the positive results of keeping sick children at the center. One reference is to a center that has a nurses' station that is staffed with professional nurses. But, she does not mention how expensive and, therefore, rare that kind of staffing is. She also refers to another center that does not isolate the sick child. This center claims that "children shed viruses before they become clinically ill. . . . We keep sick and well children together without causing excessive illness in our environment."[6]

This policy is given reinforcement in the Federal Interagency Daycare Regulations:

> The current requirement of space for isolation of the child who becomes ill has been found to be inappropriate. . . . New research shows that total isolation of the sick child does not limit contagion. Total isolation may serve only to distress the child who is ill. Space for a quiet area should be available for the rest and care of the sick child, but restricting the sick child only to this area is not recommended.[7]

One center seems unsure of what should be done. The model infant center established for one study permitted nonfeverish children with colds or upper-respiratory illnesses to attend. The staff administered medication and did not isolate symptomatic children because it believed that other children had already been exposed. The authors of the study add however, that "if he was fussy and cranky, we felt it was better for him to be at home than within the nursery for we were not equipped to cater to the special needs of an ill child."[8] And, finally, in their recommendations, the authors advise a different policy; for elsewhere they say that "there is no question that colds and mild infections are more frequent in group-care settings than they are in the home because of the constant contact with children who are temporarily ill. The child who is ill should be placed in a special room or area away from the rest of the children."[9] In other words, they recommend three policies for sick children: continued attendance and interaction; remaining at home; and isolation at the center. The reader can take her choice!

Another example from the teacher-training literature is *Day Care—Do-It-Yourself Staff Growth Program*, a hefty volume for people in early-childhood education and day care. The author addresses the health issue. She gives advice about checking children as they enter for signs of illness. She recommends that unless there are adequate isolation facilities, sick children should be sent home. She does not add that this is much more easily said than done. She gives advice about first aid, about nutrition, about detecting illnesses during the course of the morning. But, one bit of advice is rather alarming:

> Without being absurd, encourage sound health practices regarding handwashing, cooking, water play. There are other things as important as being sanitary, such as happy toilet training, learning many academic and other skills through cooking, the immense emotional importance of water play, etc. If parents want their children in a sterilized room, they shouldn't enroll them in a children's program. But we must try to be sanitary.[10]

This paragraph seems to endorse unhygienic practices. It implies that insisting on sound health practices is absurd; encouraging them is not. It implies that "happy toilet training" is not sanitary toilet training. But, it also implies, in a contradictory fashion, that teachers must "try" to be sanitary. What is a teacher to do?

One quite realistic and sensitive treatment of the health issue is the article, "Health Care Services for Children in Day Care Programs," by Julius Richmond and Juel Janis. They point out the historical, scientific, and social necessities of good health care. They also point out that despite policy statements and recommendations by the American Academy of Pediatrics, good health care and health education for the young are not likely. They cite a study in Berkeley, California, in which over one-third of the day-care centers surveyed did not have a designated health coordinator; one-fourth did not have either written health guidelines or emergency procedures; approximately one-half did not have nutrition education; and over two-thirds had no dental component. The authors are concerned that the Berkeley survey reflects health-care services in day-care centers throughout the country. "Surely," they add, "some action must be taken to address this situation."[11] Richmond and Janis find confirmation of the Berkeley data in a monograph that asserts that "in the areas of emergency preparedness, accident prevention, detection of lead paint, sanitation, (and) staff health care, day-care centers are woefully inadequate."[12]

In the Executive Summary of "Health and Safety Issues in Day Care," Susan Aronson and Peggy Pizzo conclude that there are avoidable risks in day-care centers, and the federal government pays for the exposure of young children to those avoidable risks. "Although it is not known whether the degree of risk in day-care settings is greater than, equal to, or less than the degree of risk in home surroundings, the authors contend that risk in day care can be reduced." They recommend "a national day care sanitation code" and "a child day care health and safety code."[13] Such codes, surely, would not advise teachers to encourage sound health practices without being absurd; they would not say that teachers should just *try* to be sanitary; and presumably they would not advise keeping the healthy and the sick together.

It is idealistic to hope that such codes will be written, adopted, paid for, and enforced. Therefore, medical researchers will continue to find and study health problems of day-care centers. They have known for some time of the risks to young children in group care. For instance, S.H. Gehlbach et al. did a study in 1973 of the "Spread of Disease by Fecal-Oral Route in Day Nurseries."[14] There is little evidence that matters have improved in the decade since that article was published. In fact, the infectious disease chief of the Minnesota Department of Health and other interested medical and human-service personnel are planning a national conference to try to deal with the day-care-disease issue. Dr. William Rodriguez of Children's Hospital in Washington, D.C., has said that "day care transmission is probably one of the whole nation's major health problems."[15] And Dr. Stanley Schuman, in an editorial in the *Journal of the American Medical Association*, wrote in January of 1983 that day-care infections are becoming an important public-health problem. He says that epidemics of enteric illnesses are "reminiscent of presanitation days of the 17th century."[16]

Some of the specific problems that medical researchers have dealt with have been shigellosis, a bacterial dysentery; type A viral hepatitis (VAH), which can be spread by asymptomatic carriers; hemophilus influenza type B (HIB); and cytomegalovirus. J.B. Weissman et al. wrote about shigellosis in 1974 in the *Journal of Pediatrics* in "The Role of Preschool Children and Day-Care Centers in the Spread of Shigellosis in Urban Communities."[17] In a 1975 *Lancet* article, continuing that discussion, Weissman et al. reported increasing outbreaks of shigellosis since 1972. They found that attack rates were higher in day-care centers than in elementary schools. They also found that person-to-person transmission was the usual reason for the spread, that both children and employees were infected, and that there was often a secondary spread within the households of day-care children. Their recommendations for control include: closing centers; separating the infected from the uninfected; additional hygienic precautions; and health education.[18]

These suggestions sound positive, but in actuality they are unworkable. Local, state, or federal agencies that implement and monitor even minimal standards do not have sufficient numbers of staff to enforce the closings. And a center serving working parents has a hard time closing even for holidays and renovations. Closing the center for illnesses generates other kinds of problems, for parents as well as for staff. Parents of the uninfected children do not have other available child-care facilities; parents of the infected children do not have emergency coverage. And, unfortunately, teachers in many centers are paid only for the hours that they actually work with children. Center closings would, therefore, deprive the staff of its income.

Separating the infected from the uninfected is another good recommendation, but it is an impractical one. As pointed out earlier, some authorities even recommend keeping the healthy and the sick together. In any case, space and staff costs generally make it impossible for a day-care center to have a separate supervised area for sick children. The recommendations for both hygienic precautions and health education are also rather utopian. An understaffed center cannot easily implement either of those latter suggestions.

One possible proof of the impracticality of the Weissman suggestions is that one year later, M.L. Rosenberg et al. wrote in the *American Journal of*

Epidemiology that Indian reservations, custodial institutions, and day-care centers were especially high-risk settings for the transmission of shigellosis. Rosenberg et al. looked at shigellosis more globally. They concluded that oral vaccines seem to have only limited usefulness for the control of the infection and recommend that public-health education and improved water and sewerage systems would be the best means of control.[19] They, then, see solutions in the larger scheme of public health rather than the narrower scheme of the day-care center.

R.E. Black et al., in *Pediatrics*, described a concurrent outbreak of shigellosis and giardiasis, another type of diarrhea. They found that the "prevalence of giardia lamblia in day-care children was significantly higher than . . . in age-matched children not in day-care centers. Epidemiological data suggested fecal-oral transmission of the parasite from child to child in the centers and from infected children to other family members."[20] Thus, two major causes of diarrhea, shigellosis and giardiasis, have been common to day-care children, their teachers, and their families. And, there seems to be no practical suggestion for reducing the occurrences of these diseases.

A number of studies have examined the relationship between viral hepatitis and day-care centers. In 1979, G. Storch et al. investigated an outbreak of viral hepatitis in Louisiana. They wrote that "day care center outbreaks of hepatitis are easily overlooked and may be more widespread than is currently appreciated."[21]

Clearly, these outbreaks cannot be overlooked. In a study in Maricopa County, Arizona, S.C. Hadler et al. found that 40 percent of type A viral hepatitis occurred in people associated with day-care centers. "The majority of symptomatic cases occurred in household contacts or close relatives of children who attended day care centers." The authors concluded that "day care appears to be important in the spread of hepatitis A in the United States."[22] A later study of viral A hepatitis by Hadler et al. found that outbreaks were significantly more common in centers enrolling fifty-one or more children, in centers open more than fifteen hours per day, and in for-profit centers. "The introduction of hepatitis into a center was related strongly to the number of hours open and to the size and age of enrollment, but the spread of hepatitis was related solely to the presence of children younger than two years of age."[23]

In another study in 1979, A.A. Vernon, C. Schnable, and D. Francis found associations between adults infected with hepatitis A and non-toilet-trained children. Households with non-toilet-trained children had significantly more occurrences than households with trained children.[24] Finally, a study by M.W. Benenson et al. of an outbreak in a military facility in Alaska found that over half of the cases of type A hepatitis reported there "were directly or indirectly linked to the child care facility." The researchers also found that "the length of time that a child spent at the facility appeared to increase the risk of his transmitting the hepatitis A virus to other members of his immediate household."[25]

The findings of Hadler, Vernon, and Benenson are particularly interesting in that they indicate that shorter hours of group care might reduce the public-health hazard in terms of occurrences of type A viral hepatitis. Furthermore, R.J. Silva, in an article entitled "Hepatitis and the Need for Adequate Standards in Federally Supported Day Care" concluded that, after examining the findings in three epidemiological studies, incidents of hepatitis among parents and staff could be reduced if there were higher standards of care.[26]

Several studies have dealt with hemophilus influenza type B in day-care centers. These are strains of influenza that produce conjunctivitis and influenzal meningitis. In an article in the *Journal of Pediatrics* in 1978, J.T. Ward et al. found an outbreak with episodes that were one hundred times the expected annual total.[27] Another study, by C.M. Ginsberg et al., in the *Journal of the American Medical Association*, concluded that "HIB is highly contagious in closed populations of young, susceptible infants."[28]

R.F. Pass et al. have investigated an association between HIB and cytomegalovirus (CMV). The latter, a virus of the salivary glands, is one of a group of herpes viruses that sometimes resembles mononucleosis. These researchers "found a surprisingly high rate of CMV shedding in children in a day care center" serving families of middle and upper incomes. They refer to a 1971 study by T.H. Weller that suggested that high rates of CMV infections in Scandinavian countries could be attributed "to the widespread use of child-care centers." Although the authors urge caution about generalizing from their results, they did find the association between HIB and CMV "disturbing, especially in the light of experimental evidence and clinical suspicion that CMV may impair immune responses."[29]

The medical-journal articles discussed above are representative of many similar articles about day-care diseases. This review is not intended to be an all-inclusive survey of the medical and public-health literature. However, it is clear from this sample of the medical studies that day-care centers and the children and adults connected with them are subject to a variety of germs and infections. Those germs and infections that cause gastrointestinal disease are, naturally, more rampant in centers with non-toilet-trained children and in larger centers. The influenza and hepatitis infections are present with all ages. What is most clear is that despite the fact that medical researchers have been warning about these illnesses for many years, they have not made practical, workable recommendations. Most of the conditions that cause the spread of these infections remain present. Unless higher standards of sanitation are enacted, funded, and enforced, conditions will likely remain as they have been. And, because of the gender of the caretakers and the age of the population of day-care centers, the spread of these day-care infections is, of course, to women and children first.

9 In Sickness and In Health

Medical journals call attention to some of the specific diseases that occur with frequency in day-care centers. But, they do not examine the experiences of the individual child, staff, and family. At one day-care center, Cindy was recovering from a sore throat. Her mother decided to send some cough medicine and a spoon in her lunch box. The center had a rule that the staff could not dispense medication except with the written permission of the parent and the child's physician. But, Cindy's mother was not concerned, for this was over-the-counter medication. Besides, Cindy was four and a half. She could take the medication without the teacher getting involved. The mother carefully explained to Cindy that if her throat felt worse, she should take a spoonful of the medicine. The mother told no one at the center that there was cough medicine in the lunch box.

Midmorning, an unsuspecting teacher found Cindy sitting on the floor with her friend Jeanne, giggling over an empty bottle of cough syrup. Cindy explained to the teacher that her throat hurt and that she needed to take the medicine. Since her friend Jeanne had a sore throat too, she gave some to her. Neither of Cindy's parents could be reached immediately at work, so the staff had no idea whether the girls had swallowed a teaspoonful or an entire four-ounce bottle. The director made a quick call to the nearest poison-control center. She was told that they had better take no chances. Give the children ipecac. Force them to vomit whatever they had swallowed. The staff did so. They administered the purgative. Following the directions on the bottle, they kept the children active. They ran, skipped, and jumped with them to hasten throwing up. The children finally did throw up; but, it was so sudden that they did not get to the bathroom in time. The custodian was not due to arrive for several hours. While one teacher took care of the girls, another had to clean up the mess. As the teacher was mopping the floor, another child, David, sniffed and said, "Hmm, it smells just like fried chicken!" From that time on, the staff of that day-care center found it hard to eat fried chicken without feeling a little queasy.

Once the whole ordeal was over, the staff felt exhausted and angry. They were especially angry at the parents for their carelessness about a procedure that could harm their own child as well as her classmates. They were angry, too, about the tension caused by the incident. And, they were angry because, once again, they were forced to carry out menial chores.

A fictional portrayal can also reveal the actualities of the health and sickness issue. In *The Second Stage*, Betty Friedan writes a poignant paragraph:

> And then, harassed, when the child comes down with a bug once again at school, and they call her at the office, and she can't get hold of the baby sitter, she wonders, rushing out—she'll come back later and finish the report, if the baby sitter comes, after she takes Bobby's temperature, after she talks to the doctor, or when Ralph comes home—but she wonders, "Is it worth it, working full time, always feeling so stretched, for the money I earn?"[1]

It is harassing and discouraging and makes life seem futile when this kind of thing happens to the working mother. But, what about Bobby? Betty Friedan makes no further mention of him. Assuming that Bobby is four years old and enrolled in a day-care center, what are his thoughts and his needs when he is sick?

Bobby knows, or at least suspects, what an inconvenience his illness is for his mother. He may have even complained that morning that he did not feel well, but he was cajoled and bolstered and, perhaps, told that everyone in the family had his or her job to do and Bobby's job was to go to school. And, if Bobby is typical, he tried hard for a good part of the day to stay healthy or, at least, to appear so. He knows from past experience all the problems his illnesses can create. It is okay to be ill on weekends, he thinks, but during the week an illness throws everything into confusion. Because of his level of cognitive development, because he is still egocentric, and because he has a primitive sense of his own omnipotence, he begins to think that he is a burden, an unworthy intrusion in his mother's life. He is bad if he gets sick!

Bobby also knows that as soon as he gets home, his mother will continue to try to reach the sitter. As soon as she does find someone else to stay with him, she'll have to rush back to the office and work late and it will all be Bobby's fault. If his father comes home, then Bobby will at least be with him. And, depending upon the kind of day Ralph had, and on the kind of parent he is, and on his expectations for the evening, he may or may not give Bobby the care and attention a sick child needs.

The first thing any sick child needs is nurturing care. He must be nursed, tended to, made to feel comfortable. He needs reassurance that the adults in his life are in control, that they will help him to be safe, to feel better, to recover. And so, the day-care staff, when it realizes that the child is sick, places him on a cot in the director's office. Since most day-care centers do not dispense medicine without specific written parental or medical permission, he probably will not be given any medication. He might be covered with a blanket, or, if he feels very hot, he might get a cool compress for his forehead. In all probability, the teacher who delivered him to the office will have left a large group of children with her assistant, so she really has to get back to her class. She leaves Bobby in the capable hands of the director—whom Bobby may know but certainly not as well as he knows his morning and afternoon teachers.

The director finds the emergency listing for Bobby and calls his mother at work. Mother might be presiding at a meeting, arguing in court, or performing surgery in an operating room, and be unavailable. But in this little story, as in Betty Friedan's story, mother is there and able to take the phone call. She calls her usual sitter because sometimes the sitter is able to pick Bobby up at the center in an emergency. But, she gets no answer. She has no available neighbor; her own mother and mother-in-law both have lives of their own, with full schedules of work and social commitments. Frustrated, Bobby's mother decides she has to get him herself. She puts aside her work, notifies her superior, and leaves; but, under her breath wonders if Bobby is really so sick that they couldn't have kept him at the center until the end of the day. If only her earnings matched Ralph's, she thinks, there would be a more even distribution of responsibility for Bobby. The center could call him once in a while.

She gives a quick call to the day-care center and tells them that she will be picking Bobby up in twenty minutes. The director reassures Bobby, who is relieved, of course, but also feels somewhat guilty. "I'll be very happy to see her, but," he wonders, "will she be angry with me?" The director would like to hold Bobby on her lap or read a story to him. But, if she has pressing administrative responsibilities, she must return to her desk work, essentially ignoring the sick child. Or, if she is needed for an emergency in one of the classrooms, she might be forced to leave him alone in the office.

And so, poor Bobby first felt sick; eventually he had to admit to his teachers the embarrassing and, at the same time, scary fact that he didn't feel well; he was then deposited, perhaps abruptly, in the director's office; and, finally, he witnessed several telephone calls. Can he really feel reassured about the adults in his life? Can he realize the sense of basic trust that Erik Erikson tells us all human beings need before they can become autonomous adults?[2]

Another dimension of this episode must be discussed, namely, the reaction of the day-care-center staff. What about the teacher, the director, the assistants, and, if any, the aides? It is likely that all of them first feel great sympathy for the sick child; they are in a human-service profession and are there because they want to help people and because they like children. But, it is also likely that they feel some anger toward the parents: There are so many germs and so many illnesses at the center! If only parents would keep their sick children at home, there would be less contagion! The teachers think they know what is best for Bobby and they have tried to communicate this idea to his parents, who, somehow, do not seem to absorb it. This time isn't the first that Bobby has become ill in school. No matter how often the staff talks to Bobby's parents, they continue to bring him to the center when he is not well. And, when they do keep him home for illnesses, they often do not keep him out long enough to recover fully. He comes back to the center too soon, and, with low resistance, almost immediately picks up another bug. At some point, even the most mature, sensitive, humanitarian staff will begin to transfer to the child some of the anger and resentment it feels toward the parents.

The health issue has other ramifications. Parents feel comfortable about the center, feel it is an extended family, and trust the center, so they send a sick child who should better be kept at home. This decision in turn causes the staff members to feel resentment to both child and parents, ultimately undermining the relationship with both. Anger begets anger, trust changes to mistrust, mistrust to defiance. Who do they think they are? some parents might feel. And, they continue to bring the symptomatic and sick child. The child becomes both the cause and the victim of the anger of adults at home and at school.

There are no easy answers to any of the dilemmas of day care; the illness dilemma is no exception. But Zigler and Goodman propose one such "easy answer." They suggest that high-school students and senior citizens be trained in child development. "They would provide a valuable resource as regular child care workers and for emergency care, such as when a child or parent becomes ill."[3]

This policy recommendation is unworkable and, in fact, sad. It suggests that teenagers and senior citizens are both available and willing to be called upon in an emergency. It implies that their responsibilities can be readily interrupted. It also assumes that senior citizens and high-school students *want* to take care of sick children on an emergency basis. And, it implies that if they are available and willing, it will be good for the child. A sick child, as we have seen, is frightened and confused. It is not hard to imagine his response to the arrival of an unknown elderly lady or gentleman, or of an unfamiliar adolescent, also ill at ease, frightened, and confused.

The success of the foster-grandparent program in one area in no way guarantees success in other areas. For example, one day-care director went to a meeting of a local senior-citizen group. Most of the people at the meeting were women and most had come to play cards. When the director talked about children during naptime and how they all needed an extra pat on the back or a book read or some adult comfort and suggested that providing that sort of care might interest some of the group, several ladies laughed. They had put in their time with the young, they said. Also, they were insulted about the request for volunteering. "Everyone wants us to do something," one woman said, "but no one wants to pay us." Perhaps Zigler and Goodman propose to pay teenagers and senior citizens a retainer to keep them available, but that would be a hefty expenditure in an already underbudgeted, labor-intensive service.

There is a far more serious assumption underlying the Zigler and Goodman proposal, namely, that some training in child development can make people into child-care workers or persons capable of taking care of sick children. It is yet another example of how little value is placed upon the professionals in the child-care field. And that low esteem results, as we see again and again, because child care has always been women's work, and, therefore, is of low professional status. No one would ever suggest that with a little training our teenagers and senior citizens could service our computers or research legal cases in an emergency. Yet, sensitive experts, like Zigler and Goodman, make such a proposal for the emergency care of the young.

The most serious flaw in this suggestion is its lack of concern for the child. A sick child needs nurturing, warmth, security, and love. Having a substitute list of caregivers, whether they are teenagers or senior citizens, and contacting that substitute in an emergency, when the child is both physically and psychologically weak, is not what is best for a child.

Perhaps the solution to the problem of the care of sick children depends, as so much in the day-care field does, on a monetary solution. A workshop at the National Association for the Education of Young Children, in November of 1982, was entitled "Industry meets the challenge—reduced absenteeism and increased productivity result from a sick-child home-care program."[4] The program, in Tucson, Arizona, claims to provide skilled aides to take care of an ill child in the child's own home. Aides are screened and must be healthy, honest, and dependable; they must love children. They participate in six weeks of intensive training that includes health assessment, common childhood ailments, health and child-care skills, first aid and cardiopulmonary resuscitation, care and comfort measures, growth and development, and appropriate activities.[5] One might question whether all of these skills can be learned in six weeks. One might suspect that the turnover of aides is high because they work sporadically and are paid the minimum wage. And one might wonder about the feelings of an ill child left with a strange sitter/health aide. But, the program is described as reducing absenteeism and increasing productivity—a recurrent theme of center-based day care. Whether the children are fictional like Friedan's Bobby or real like those in Tucson, their needs, even when they are ill, are subordinate to those of adults. Solutions are found not because they are best for children but because of their effect on the bottom line.

10 Research and Reality

For more than a decade, developmental psychologists have been studying the effects of day care on young children. Researchers have studied infants and toddlers, and they have studied three-to-five-year olds. They have studied children in their homes, in laboratories, and in day-care centers. They have used existing centers and they have used new centers established expressly for research. They have observed children with their parents and with their peers. They have watched children interact—or refuse to interact—with familiar caretakers and with strangers. They have done naturalistic observations, and they have administered standardized tests. They have compared home-raised children and center-raised children. They have conducted research with poor children and with middle-class children. They have looked at variables ranging from caretaker stability to peer influence and at outcome measures ranging from mother-child attachment to intelligence. They have used all currently available methods to try to determine the social, emotional, and cognitive effects of day care on children.[1] One major study has looked carefully at day-care centers to try to identify those measurable factors in the day-care experience that lead to optimal growth for young children.[2] The research on the major outcome measures—attachment, social development, and intelligence—has been reviewed thoroughly by several scholars. Two of the most comprehensive reviews are Belsky and Steinberg, "The Effects of Day Care: A Critical Review,"[3] updated in Belsky, Steinberg, and Walker, "The Ecology of Day Care";[4] and Michael Rutter, "Social and Emotional Consequences of Day Care for Preschool Children."[5] Because of the thoroughness of those reviews, this chapter will not review the literature. Instead it will briefly summarize the findings.

In studies of attachment, children who have entered day-care centers as infants, toddlers, or preschoolers have exhibited secure ties to their mothers.[6] The most common way for researchers to appraise the degree of mother-child attachment is a laboratory procedure, the Ainsworth Strange Situation.[7] In this paradigm, the child and the mother are brought to a laboratory and the child is subjected to varying degrees of stress by separating her from her mother and by introducing strange adults. Investigators look at the child's behavior in exploring the new environment; at the amount of and duration of the child's distress when her mother ignores her or departs abruptly; at the child's interactions with a strange adult; and at the child's reaction during reunion.

The Strange Situation procedure has been used in numerous experiments. In comparison with home-reared children, day-care children show the same kinds of emotional bonds to their mothers. And, despite long hours in substitute care, day-care children have stronger attachments to their own mothers than they have to their caretakers; that is, in these laboratory situations, they are more upset when their mothers leave than when their teachers do. When they need to be comforted, day-care children still look to their mothers for that comfort. And they respond positively to reunions with their mothers.[8] One recent review of the attachment studies has concluded that the "emotional development of young children is little influenced by their day care experience."[9]

In studies of social development day-care children seem less dependent on adults and interact more with their peers than do their home-raised counterparts. There is some suggestion that day-care children have more anxiety with strange adults, but they interact more with strange children. There is also some evidence that it is not day-care as such but, rather, the community setting and the specific policies of the program that influence the social behavior of the day-care child.[10]

On standardized tests of intelligence and cognition, researchers have found more social-class differences among children than day-care/home-care differences. In fact, there seems to be an advantage for lower-socio-economic-class children in day care. They score higher in tests for cognition than do matched home-raised children, although most differences tend to disappear in early elementary school.

Researchers, then, have found little evidence that day care harms children. Nevertheless, it is important to interpret these findings with caution, for there are intrinsic limitations to the research. Although the research finds no damage, it *proves* nothing. Science cannot *prove* a negative; it cannot prove that an experience is *not* detrimental. The research *does* indicate that with the limited testing methods available, and in limited settings, there appear to be no significant differences in limited outcome measures between center-reared and home-reared children.

One major limitation is that most of the research has dealt with a narrow selection of outcome measures, or dependent variables. Research has been concerned mainly with attachment, as measured in the strange situation, and with intelligence, as measured by standardized tests. Both of these research techniques place children in unnatural, artificial situations, where the reality of their lives is secondary to the reality, and sometimes the stress, of the testing situation. As Belsky and Steinberg point out, "Most studies on the effects of day care utilize either laboratory experiments or psychological tests. In each instance, the generalizability of the results to behavior in real life settings of home, neighborhood, preschool, and school can be . . . seriously questioned."[11] Rutter echoes this warning. "The range of psychological outcome variables in most investigations has been so narrow and so limited that it would be misleading to conclude that their negative findings rule out the presence of damage."[12]

Another limitation to the research is that it has lacked the random assignments necessary for validation. Most of the children sampled are in day care or in home care because their family circumstances are different, with different goals and expectations. Thus, there are many factors contributing to the child's behavior and performance. To attribute similarities or differences to the center or the home experience alone is to deny the influence of many other factors in the child's life. Some researchers have attempted to counteract those flaws by selecting control groups from day-care waiting lists, thus providing for some commonality among parents: they all want to use day care.[13] However, this technique introduces another variable. The control group, on the waiting lists, is made up of children whose parents are dissatisfied about either their work or their child-care arrangements and are seeking some change. In seeking a valid sample, the researchers introduce another variable.

Another limitation to the research is that it has been limited largely to short-term effects. Until more longitudinal studies are completed, there is no way of knowing what long-term, so-called sleeper effects may be due to attendance at a day-care center.

Finally, the research has been limited to university-based, high-quality settings. One example of a high-quality setting is the Tremont Street Infant Center, a special day-care center created for the Jerome Kagan, Richard Kearsley, Philip Zelazo landmark study.[14] The center serviced thirty-three infants between the ages of three-and-a-half and five-and-a-half months. A control group of sixty-seven infants was reared at home. Thirty-two of the control group were matched to the day-care children in age, sex, ethnicity, and social class. All of the children were from intact, working-class and middle-class Caucasian and Chinese families, living in a working-class section of Boston, Massachusetts. The center, the Tremont Street Infant Center, was well staffed in terms of numbers, with a ratio of one adult to three in the infant group and, as the children grew older, one adult to five for toddlers. There was unusual staff consistency, for in its five years of operation, all but two of the original staff remained. The authors hypothesize that generous salaries and an emphasis on the importance of staff contributed to this stability. Long tenure, adequate salaries, and respected status are, of course, atypical for most day-care workers.

Subjects in the study were assessed at two-month intervals from three and one-half months to thirteen and one-half months and again at twenty months and twenty-nine months. The researchers were concerned with five major characteristics: attentiveness, excitability, reactivity to others, attachment, and, later, cognitive functioning. After extensive observations, tests, and data analysis, the researchers did not find "much support for the view that quality group care outside the home has an important effect on the young child's development."[15] The authors conclude that "attendance at a day care center staffed by conscientious and nurturant adults during the first two-and-one-half years of life does not seem to produce a psychological profile very much different from the one created by rearing totally at home. . . . Day care, when reasonably and conscientiously implemented, does not seem to have hidden psychological dangers."[16]

The important phrases to stress here are *conscientious and nurturant adults* and *day care reasonably and conscientiously implemented*. The bulk of the research on day care has been carried out in high-quality settings, and, therefore, findings cannot be generalized to the entire world of day care.

Because of all the limitations—in methodology, in sample selection, in longevity of studies, in quality of settings—it is hasty to draw conclusions or to make sweeping generalizations. What is needed is more research and research of a different kind. Rutter has suggested that research should move from crude comparisons of home rearing versus day care and must "determine the specific effects of the various aspects of care in specific circumstances."[17]

One major study has attempted to determine what specific features are related to specific outcomes in day care. "In 1974, the need was clear for studying a comprehensive set of center characteristics, a sample of centers and children likely to be affected by federal policy, and a design adequate to separate the effects, on quality of care, of ratio, group size, and other characteristics, to relate them to costs, and to assess their impact on center day care nationally."[18] This need created the mandate for another landmark study of day care, the National Day Care Study by Richard Ruopp et al. for Abt Associates. The study, which cost a total of eight million dollars, took five years to complete.[19] Its major objective was to gather empirical data in three different areas: "(1) the quality of day care in federally subsidized programs; (2) the cost per child of the day care provided; and (3) the potential quality/cost trade-offs . . . (for) alternative formulations of federal day care regulations."[20] The Abt study looked at fifty-seven day-care centers in Atlanta, Detroit, and Seattle. The cities were chosen for geographic and demographic diversity; the centers were all recipients of federal funds. To assess the effects of various components of the day-care center, researchers used naturalistic observations of both children and adults; and they administered standardized tests to children.

They found three major variables that correlated with higher-quality care. Total group size was the most significant variable; that is, children functioned better in smaller groups than in larger ones. They showed less aimless wandering, interacted more with teachers, and performed better on standardized tests. Although the ratio of adult to child was important, it was not as significant as the size of the group. Thus, a group composed of one teacher and eight children functioned better than a group with two teachers and sixteen children; but the latter was better than four teachers with thirty-two children. The Abt group found this variable significant because it suggested an improvement that could be achieved without raising costs.

The second major finding of the Abt study was that staff ratios of one adult to eight, nine, or ten enrolled children were adequate for three-to-five-year olds. They based this position on hard data that included average daily attendance figures and cost-benefit analyses; that is, a ratio of eight children to one teacher may be ideal but, because of attendance statistics, ten to one becomes acceptable as an economic trade-off.

The third major finding of the Abt National Day Care Study was that the general educational level of the caretaker and the length of her experience were not of great significance; but, some training in child development was. Teachers who had had specific training in relevant courses interacted more with children and less often with other teachers. They spent less time in management and housekeeping functions. This finding, too, becomes an important factor in cost-benefit analysis. High-school graduates with some training would, of course, command lower salaries than college graduates.

The National Day Care Study is important in that it was the beginning of a serious examination of quality. It recognized and called attention to the fact that day care is an area that must be regulated and that it is the responsibility of the federal government to set minimal standards for that regulation. In addition, it recognized that group size is an important variable for the success of the program. This finding should counteract some of the tendencies of for-profit or financially struggling centers to exceed recommended enrollment to maximize incomes. The finding on teacher training is also an important one. It should silence those who advise the use of volunteers to assume child-care responsibilities. But, it is unrealistic to expect that the National Day Care Study's three variables would be adequate, in and of themselves, to create high-quality day-care centers.

The Abt study is concerned primarily with cost-benefits and bottom lines. It cannot capture the reality, the texture of a day-care center. In its concern for bottom lines, the study has reduced much of the day-care experience to statistical abstractions. These abstractions, these numbers, are reminiscent of the suggestion that one particluar person, of the right age, sex, and occupation, in a particular town in Iowa, is all that is needed to elect a president of the United States. However, like an election, life in a day-care center—for children and for adults—is hardly an abstraction. Life in a day-care center is made up of good days and bad days. It is made up of perfectly smooth and tranquil mornings that become chaotic for no apparent reason. The converse can be true, too. Chaotic mornings can suddenly turn into well-directed, productive ones. Teachers who work in day care know all this. They know that children, like adults, are sometimes happy and sometimes sad. They know that even a child who is securely attached to her mother can take a long time to recover and resume play after a confusing experience.

For these reasons, some teachers look with skepticism on the Abt National Day Care Study recommendations for ratios based on attendance rather than enrollment. The teacher in the one-to-ten ratio has a very different perspective from the researcher who comes in with stopwatch and check sheets. The teacher knows that life in the day-care center goes on for ten hours a day, five days a week, fifty weeks a year. On the days when all the children show up, ten children to one adult is a hard reality for the teacher and for the children. The teacher cannot say to her children that because everyone is here today they will have to change their schedule and postpone making oatmeal cookies. She cannot be sure that Johnny will not have a temper tantrum or that Sally will not have a toileting accident. She will not be able to comfort Jane if she becomes distraught in the block corner.

That teacher is probably more in agreement with the results of a modest, less sophisticated study than the Abt one. In one survey of day-care workers, only 60 percent of those who worked with ratios of *less* than one to ten felt that *they* had sufficient time for individual work with children. Seventy-eight percent of the proprietary centers in their sample had ratios of over one to ten, and it was staff in those centers who were most likely to perceive children as a source of tension.[21]

Most teachers are likely to perceive discrepancies between reality and research, between the actual work of caring for children for long hours and the statistical abstractions of the scientist. In fact, a task force on teacher-preparation programs concludes that "traditional quantitative and experimental methodologies are inadequate for the nature of the child care field and its research needs."[22] As David Elkind has pointed out, "When researchers and practitioners interact, they lack a common language and a common outlook on what is important and upon what is real."[23] Practitioners must urge researchers to incorporate more systematic observational studies, fewer removals from the classroom to the laboratory. Researchers must "enrich (their) assessment procedures to measure aspects of children's development not covered by eye movement recordings and IQ scores, increase the scope of background factors studied to reflect broader influences on children's lives, and invent or select research designs that will more appropriately evaluate the effects of . . . interventions on children's development."[24]

Practitioners must become more involved in research design. They must demand studies that help them take better care of children, studies that shed light on aggression, on anger, on loneliness, on cognition. Developmental research is important because it can help adults understand children better, not because it evaluates. When research is used to evaluate, to predict, to make judgments, it is less useful than when it is used to understand, to interpret what children are saying and what they are doing. Developmental psychology must move from the laboratory to the field. It must refine its methods of systematic observation. Then, perhaps, researchers and practitioners will find a common language and will be able to reconcile research with reality.

11 Day-Care Advocates and Critics

There are sharp differences between the critics of day care and the advocates of it. Each side seems to take a firm, entrenched position, so that attitudes become polarized and there is little opportunity for dialogue. One example of that polarization is seen in *Families at Work*. This book describes the results of a survey done by Louis Harris Associates for General Mills. In one section, the survey asks if it is a good thing or a bad thing for families if "day care centers and other child care outside the home become more common."[1]

The question was asked of a number of groups, but the answers of two groups are particularly interesting. One group, called *feminists*, were leaders active in women's rights organizations. Ninety-four percent of this group responded that out-of-home child care was good for families. Only 4 percent saw it as bad.

Another group, defined by the pollsters as leaders in the "profamily movement," and called *traditionalists*, responded in the opposite way. Only 13 percent of the traditionalists saw more widespread child-care services as good for families. Eighty-one percent of this group saw it as a bad thing. Yet, it is not just the so-called righteous right,[2] the profamily, traditionalist voices that have been raised against day care. For instance, Valerie Suransky in *The Erosion of Childhood* makes a passionate plea against most forms of day care and makes it far from the perspective of right-wing conservatism. She writes:

> With the rapid rise of the daycare movement over the past decade and the inevitable absorption of women into a corporate economy, attendant modes of alienation have been produced by a bureaucratically-organized hierarchical division of labor, where the female "worker" now occupies the lowest echelon of power and status. The current call for free and universal daycare should not be viewed as a progressive or radical answer to the social needs of women in a society entering the work force seeking the equalization of opportunity; rather, the daycare phenomenon merely extends and exascerbates (sic) the corporate paradigm, thereby contributing to the *maintenance*, not the *transformation* of the social order (italics in original).[3]

But, not all of the concerns about day care have emerged from opposite political poles. As was stressed in chapter 10 many developmental psychologists advise caution about the unquestioned use of positive research results. They point out the various limitations of that research.

Other voices of caution have perhaps been more eloquent. Selma Fraiberg, the clinician and researcher, in *Every Child's Birthright* states: "We do not need to 'prove' that such programs can be damaging to many children. When a child spends 11 to 12 hours of his waking day in the care of indifferent custodians, no parent and no educator can say that the child's development is being promoted or enhanced, and common sense tells us that children are harmed by indifference."[4]

Fraiberg drew on her own clinical experience and her research on attachment, bonding, and separation. She criticized a political and economic system that forced young welfare mothers to take menial jobs while their children were sent to institutional day-care centers. She pointed out some of the pitfalls of day care for young children. Every child, she said, needs a special adult, an adult who thinks that child is absolutely special. In a day-care center it is impossible for even the best-trained, best-suited caregivers to view several children as that special.

Fraiberg pointed out that in some day-care centers there are long periods each day for many children when none of the adults present is familiar to the child. She discussed the potential sadness for a child when she becomes attached to one caregiver who leaves, makes another attachment, and then sees that second important person leave. At some point, the child stops making attachments, stops depending on the adults in her environment. According to psychoanalytic theory, that child is not likely to be able to make the lasting commitments and attachments necessary for human love. Looking at children at each stage of early childhood, Fraiberg wrote "that all children at all ages need stability, continuity, and predictability in their human partnerships for love, for trust, for learning and self-worth."[5]

"By the time the baby is six months old, love and valuation of his mother take on poignant meaning; even minor separations from her can be distressing. . . . Between the ages of six months and three years, children who are strongly attached to their parents will show distress and even panic when they are separated from their parents and left with strangers[6]. . . . When preschool children are separated from their mothers for 9 to 10 hours there is a point of diminishing returns in the nursery day, and finally a point where no educational benefits accrue to the child. By afternoon, after nap time, restlessness, tearfulness, whininess, or lassitude become epidemic in the group of 3 to 6 year olds. Even the most expert teachers have difficulty in sustaining the program and restoring harmony. What we see is longing for mother and home."[7] Thus, Fraiberg finds the full-time day-care experience a difficult one for children ranging in age from infancy to six years old.

Every Child's Birthright was decried by feminists. Fraiberg's very human plea for considering the children was ignored by the more strident voices of the feminist movement. Instead her book was seen as "one for the 'biology is destiny' fans," as one sending women back into the home and the nursery.[8]

In the same year that F. Fraiberg's book was published, Sally Provence, Audrey Naylor, and June Patterson wrote *The Challenge of Daycare.* The book is a full and detailed description of a pilot program at Yale University undertaken with much federal support. The Yale program was a research and demonstration project that integrated center care and home care and provided medical, psychological, and social supports to family and staff. In other words, it was about as close to ideal as a program could be. But, of course, it was only a demonstration project; so when the funds ran out it was discontinued. Because of its expense, it could not be duplicated.

There is one telling chapter called "Considerations in the Choice of Daycare." It says:

> When adults have a fair capacity to be parents, their young children do best when cared for mainly by them[9]. . . . Group care, even under the best circumstances, is stressful for very young children[10]. . . . If some kind of substitute care during the first year cannot be avoided because the mother must work, part-time will ordinarily be better for the child than full-time[11]. . . . In contrast to the natural family setting and activities, how artificial is the daycare center and what it can provide! It is very difficult to duplicate in the center more than a few of the experiences most appropriate for the toddler, experiences that he could have at home without anyone giving the matter a moment's thought[12]. . . . The child from one to three is not by nature a highly suitable member of a large group, whether of similar or diverse ages, and difficulties appear to magnify as the group increases in size[13]. . . . Length of day, also, is still very much the issue, for separation reactions become more acute as the day lengthens and fatigue decreases coping ability.[14]

The authors state that they are not writing the book to be for or against day care. But it is clear that when research is combined with practice and with a search for excellence, there are caveats about extended group care for children through age three.

Other child-development professionals have also expressed warnings. In *The Hurried Child*, Elkind says, "The demands of two parents working should not blind us to children's built-in limitations of responsibility, achievement, and loyalty."[15] Elsewhere, in that book, he speaks of the difficulties children have when separating "from people and things they consider their own." For they "believe that they are responsible for parental separation. . . . Some act he or she committed. . . . caused the separation."[16] Furthermore, he explains that:

> Children need time to explore in a responsive environment in order to acquire a healthy sense of initiative. When children are hurried from one day care center or caretaker to another, there is no time to explore, and when the environment is not responsive—parents are too busy or too tired to respond to their children's questions—the children's sense of doubt about

> themselves and their exploratory actions far exceeds the healthy sense of initiative, the sense that it is okay to be curious and wondering. The sense of doubt established in early childhood provides a lifelong orientation that can inhibit the young person's initiative in his or her dealings with the social as well as the physical world.[17]

Stll another child-development professional uses stronger words. Burton White, in "Should You Stay Home With Your Baby?" cites the literature on attachment and the results of research and says that even if research has found no harm in day care, it has not "addressed the question of what is very good for young children. . . . Put simply, after more than 20 years of research on how children develop well, I [White] would not think of putting a child of my own into any substitute-care program on a full-time basis, especially a center-based program." He cannot recommend "full-time substitute care during the first years of life . . . except under extraordinary circumstances."[18]

Finally, another warning must be mentioned. In *Day Care: Serving Preschool Children*, a handbook published in 1974 by the Office of Child Development, there is one section virtually tucked away:

> Any responsible person involved in day care must recognize the danger that it may hold for children and families. Enthusiasm for the many potential benefits should be tempered by the realization that day care can be a source of harm, and that a good program requires a commitment to constant thoughtfulness and careful monitoring.
>
> The most obvious danger is that the child may be neglected, abused physically or emotionally, or exposed to unsafe or unhealthy conditions. But, there are more subtle possibilities for damage. Some unusually sensitive or immature children have difficulty separating from their parents; some have trouble accommodating to group activities and noise; and some with developmental difficulties may find it even harder to progress in the relatively hurried, tense atmosphere of many day-care programs. Other conditions may also put stress on any child: subjection to a routine; exposure to other, more aggressive children; exposure to different backgrounds and different languages; and perhaps the most difficult, the breaks in continuity that occur more or less frequently when caregivers change. Children may thus have to deal with a series of emotional attachments and separations. They may withhold their emotions and become suspicious of adults, or they may learn to make only superficial attachments.[19]

In a handbook of 160 pages, designed to help people establish and run quality day-care centers, two paragraphs are inserted in the first chapter. All of the issues pointed out, however, have been and still are worrisome to many children's advocates.

It is ironic that many voices that ordinarily champion children are, by and large, hushed when it comes to exposing the realities of center-based day care. In particular, many early-childhood professional practitioners, those informed adults who actually *do* experience day care, have been reluctant to call attention to the drawbacks of institutional day care.

There are several possible reasons for this reluctance. One reason is that early-childhood practitioners know that, for some children, life in an institution, or in any monitored group setting, even for long hours, is preferable to life at home with an inadequate or unhappy or abusive parent or caretaker. These professionals understand that a day-care center is often a place where children are given rich opportunities for physical, social, and cognitive growth. It is sometimes the place where developmental lags or handicaps are first detected, diagnosed, and treated.

There are other reasons for educators to maintain silence about the negatives. Some early-childhood educators have, in fact, seen good centers. They have seen facilities run by capable, competent, often self-sacrificing professionals who have the strengths to withstand the pressures of their work and avoid bitterness and burnout. They have seen centers provide good space, hygienic conditions, careful programs, all under the direction of nurturant, thoughtful teachers. But, these centers tend to be very expensive, either to the participating parents or to the sponsoring agency. Many higher-quality centers involve leadership from active, concerned parents. It is another irony of the day-care situation that those parents who need day care the most, the single parents and those who must have two incomes to buy life necessities, are often the ones with the least energy and time to spend on the day-care center. Yet, without parental control and input, it is unlikely that any center can be a truly good one.

Another reason for the reluctance of many early-childhood educators to speak out against day care is that they do not want to jeopardize current funding, minimal though it is. They fear that their opposition or complaint will only worsen the situation, not better it. Ultimately, their criticism might lead not to better but to worse services for children. In fact, their criticism could provide ammunition to opponents of all governmental participation in child-care services. To use an unfortunate metaphor, they are afraid to see the baby thrown out with the bath water.

Furthermore, early-childhood educators have a special interest in parents, and especially in mothers. They, of all people, understand the dilemmas that young mothers face in their attempts to balance home and career. They frequently deal with feelings of parental guilt and inadequacy and see the effects of these feelings on children. Therefore, they do not speak out against day care because they do not want to intensify parental doubts and conflicts.

Still another reason for silence might be the sense of betrayal that early-childhood professionals would feel toward their colleagues and their clients. The field is a helping profession, with many dedicated people, especially women, in it. The last thing many early-childhood practitioners want to do is make things more difficult for their colleagues, for children, or for parents. Any criticism of day care might be seen as a betrayal of all three.

Most early-childhood educators are optimists. They believe that their intervention can make a difference in the lives of children. Therefore, instead of cursing the darkness, they light candles. They work for relatively low wages. They consult for no fee. They write papers that suggest improvements to programs and facilities that will not increase budgets. They attend and sponsor workshops and training sessions on curriculum and on burnout. They accept the reality of the day-care center and try to improve upon it as best they can. Many early-childhood educators perceive their role as one that must conceptualize quality and then must work for the achievement of it.

However, some early-childhood educators do not have such idealistic motivations. They have institutional affiliations that give them a vested interest in the continuation and expansion of day-care services. The schools where they trained and where many now teach continue to train workers in the field. It is important that they believe in what they are doing and in the viability of the profession. Their careers are dependent on institutional child care. Therefore, they convince themselves, and the public, that day care is in the best interests of the child. The day-care center, some maintain, can be a place for the hastening of independence in children. They sometimes lose sight of the fact that hastening development is no more appropriate in children than it is anywhere else in nature.

When confronted with the criticisms, the drawbacks, some early-childhood educators reply that parents have no other choices. They may be early-childhood educators but, like so many involved in the politics of day care, they place the needs of the parents ahead of those of the child. When questioned about the health issue, some educators maintain that early exposure to many of the day-care-center-rampant bacterial and viral infections will produce immunity to those diseases in adulthood. This belief is a rather lame justification for group care, especially when it is used by people interested in the health of young children. Thus, some professionals are motivated by self-interest, by self-perpetuation of their careers. They insist that center-based care is a good thing for young children. And, they try to deny any negatives while they vilify the opposition.

In addition to training institutions, there are professional associations that encourage loyalty to and defense of the concepts of center-based care. In some cases, professional organizations have become lobbies for the child-care industry. These associations, often with the excuse that they want to improve the lot of children, have welcomed to their membership all programs that serve children. It seems to be a case of "If you can't beat them, let them join." Thus, they have given professional status and credibility to the entrepreneurs, the franchisers, the for-profit day-care centers and the drop-in centers. Some workshops at the 1982 Conference of the National Association for the Education of Young Children (NAEYC) are examples of this umbrella policy of acceptance. One workshop was called "Yes, child care CAN be profitable!" This workshop dealt with the interdependence of staff scheduling, ratios, profit-loss, and budgeting. As evident in examinations of staff and budgetary issues (chapters 5 and 7), profits for day-care centers have to be at the expense of children, of staff, of parents, of space, and/or of program. Another workshop was called "The World's Fair Child Care Project—an initiation into casual care." Another was called "Regulation of a new phenomenon—drop-in child care." One of the presenters at the latter workshop is identified as a representative of Check-a-Child, Inc. Thus, for-profit care, casual care, and drop-in care become associated with the *education* of young children. Yet, the dehumanizing aids mentioned earlier (chapter 2) must be a necessity for many of these facilities for the casual care of children.

Clearly, entrepreneurial enterprises are given status and professional credibility by the very association that is devoted to children and their teachers. "The expressed purpose of NAEYC is to serve and act on behalf of the needs and rights of young children, with the primary focus on the provision of educational services and resources to adults who work with and for children."[20]

Professional practitioners in the early-childhood field might heed the warnings of Fraiberg and Suransky, of Elkind and White. They might rethink their acceptance of such enterprises as Check-a-Child, Inc.; and they might rethink their unqualified espousal of center-based care as the best alternative for the eighties. They might raise their voices, too, and admit the shortcomings, the realities, of center-based care. As part of the day-care lobby, they must become less defensive about, less protective of, center-based care. Instead of standing squarely in defense of day care, with no reservations, they must acknowledge the weaknesses, the limitations. They must enter into a dialogue with day-care critics and attempt to lessen some of the anger and polarization that now occurs. They must stop being part of what Woolsey calls the "interest group pied pipers."[21] Until and unless they do, day-care centers are likely to remain underfunded, teachers are likely to remain underpaid, and children are likely to become dehumanized. Women and children will continue to be last, not first.

12 Child-Based Solutions

Many people propose the expansion of day-care services as the major solution to a number of diverse social problems, including the problem of child care for working parents. Woolsey, in "Pied Piper Politics and the Child-Care Debate," has called day-care advocates a "diverse coalition" that "includes, among others, 'workfare' conservatives, unemployed teachers, the women's movement, professionals in child development and social welfare, and entrepreneurs looking for a new growth industry,"[1] Few people, in fact, advocate day care, or alternative arrangements, as a solution to children's needs. Rather, they advocate children's services as a solution to the needs of adults. Some parents seek child care so that they can work. Some government officials and policymakers see child-care services as a means to get large numbers of women off the welfare rolls. And, some members of the early-childhood establishment see child care as a necessity for their own careers.

But some of these advocates seem confused about the various child-care services available in the United States. Many people, including parents and policymakers do not distinguish between play groups, family day care, nursery schools, or day-care centers. For instance, a population report issued by the U.S. Bureau of the Census, called *Trends in Child Care Arrangements of Working Mothers*, states that "For the purposes of this report, the term 'group care center' includes all types of child care, day care, and group care centers in addition to nursery schools, preschools, and kindergartens."[2] In fact, there are large differences between these programs, their costs, and the services they provide.

Simple definitions of child-care options are rarely sufficient. To be accurate, observers should actually be present, should physically experience the atmosphere for the same length of time that children do—for words can not adequately capture the reality of facilities for children. The following brief definitions and descriptions are made with that limitation in mind.

Play groups are generally informal arrangements of several children with either a parent—usually the mother—or a sitter in charge. They often take place on a rotating basis in different homes, with the families alternating the care. Thus, they are a kind of babysitting cooperative. Because they are informal, they are not subject to regulation or direction, and, therefore, can be as appropriate as the individual parents or sitters make them. They can be lovely opportunities for small children to have social experiences with other children; they can offer pleasant learning opportunities; they can be a cooperative function of families; they can be a challenge and a learning experience for parents as they act as teachers to their own and to other people's children; and, of course, they can provide care for children so that parents have some discretionary time.

Because of the involvement of parents in this kind of play group, there appear to be few risks for the child. Presumably, parents who become involved in cooperative play groups share many of the values and goals of the other parents. Thus, the experience of the child is likely to be consistent: a small group of children with a small number of familiar adults, most of whom agree about methods of child care.

Of course, the play group is hardly the solution for the two-parent working family, for if it is informal and relies on rotating parents to provide care, then it is not adequate for the purposes of most working couples. Family day care, another option, offers better services for working parents. It is also the first choice of most parents.[3]

Family day care is a system, sometimes regulated and sometimes not, in which one person, occasionally with additional support, takes care of a small group of children in her home. It is often as pleasant as a play group for a young child. It can be a homey atmosphere with a warm and caring adult and a small group of friends. Conversely, it can be detrimental to children.[4] If the family-day-care provider is not conscientious, and if parents do not exercise their rights and obligations to enforce standards of safety and good care, then even that situation can be hazardous. A family-day-care home can be unsafe and chaotic. It can include many small children crowded into limited space, with insufficient ventilation and fire exits. It can have small babies propped with bottles or toddlers glued to television soap operas. It can involve one driver with five children riding in a car with no seat belts. It can involve a caregiver who suffers from fatigue, isolation, and exploitation. She might be taking in children to support her own family and so she frequently has her own children present. And, she might show a preference for her own. Or, if her children resent the presence of other children in their home, they might become aggressive to the perceived intruders. With little training or experience in the management of these normal developmental issues, the provider might act inappropriately with both her own children and her charges. Abuses can happen in the family-day-care system even if the home is registered, for few monitoring agencies have the staff or the funds to carefully check on each registered home in their jurisdictions. More often agencies respond to complaints of infringements but cannot prevent infringements before they occur.

According to the National Day Care Home Study, in 1975 there were over five million children in family day care with nonrelatives for at least ten hours a week.[5] The largest percentage in the National Day Care Home

Study, 94 percent were in unregulated homes; the other children in the study were in either regulated homes or in family-day-care homes that were sponsored by another agency or system. The regulated homes were licensed or registered with the appropriate state agency.

The study looked at 352 family-day-care homes. All of the providers were women. The largest age group cared for was toddlers, with infants, preschoolers, and school-age children about evenly represented. The study found that most homes, whether regulated or not, complied with group-size recommendations. In fact, there were larger enrollments in sponsored homes than in unregulated ones. Women doing family day care did not need external enforcement for group size; they voluntarily restricted the numbers of children in their care. If, according to this study, regulatory status was not a significant influence on group size, it was on caregiver interactions with children. The study found that those caretakers who had sponsored homes spent more time interacting with children than did caretakers in regulated homes. Caretakers in unsponsored or unregulated homes spent the least amount of time interacting with children. Furthermore, the most positive interactions were found in sponsored homes.[6]

The National Day Care Home Study is reassuring about the enrollments of the family-day-care homes sampled. And, it indicates that with some sponsorship caretakers can apparently meet many of the needs of small groups of children. But, the study does raise some serious issues, issues that are inescapable in discussions of all forms of child care. The average fee paid by parents was $0.59 per hour; and the net wage for family-day-care providers was $1.25 per hour. S. Fosburg, one of the authors of the final report of the study, did some calculations that indicate the wage-earning status of family-day-care providers. He based his estimates on the minimum wage of 1977, $2.65 per hour, and the fees family-day-care providers charged. He found that charges for unregulated homes would have to increase 190 percent to provide caregivers with a minimum wage. The charges in regulated and sponsored homes would have to increase 59 percent and 28 percent, respectively, to bring the providers up to minimum wage.[7]

Of course, all of the providers were women! Not surprisingly, the care that most parents want for their children is yet another system for the exploitation of women. That exploitation, that treatment of women and their work as worthless, as well-below minimal standards, must ultimately have an impact on the children being cared for and on their views of women.

In fact, the family-day-care provider has many of the same difficulties that the day-care-center teacher has: low salary, low status, thankless work, health risks, and few options for career advancement. Day-care-center teachers at least work with colleagues and usually work in six-hour shifts. The family-day-care provider works in isolation and often must work from early morning until midevening. Parents expect that the day-care provider will be available for emergency evening, and even overnight, care. There seems to be little consideration for the realities of the provider's life.

Thus, play groups and family day care, although often equated, are quite different kinds of programs. There is confusion, too, about the differences between nursery schools and day-care centers. One reason for that confusion is that both nursery schools and day-care centers fall under the general heading of early-childhood education. Both are outgrowths of the kindergarten and day-nursery movements that, in turn, were responses by nineteenth-century reformers to the industrial revolution and to widespread immigration.[8]

Before the Industrial Revolution and its consequent division of labor and transfer of the workplace from home to factory, the care and teaching of most children was carried on within the home. In the agrarian economy, childrearing was a family function, along with other service functions like the care of the sick and the elderly. With society in an upheaval and with traditional roles and responsibilities changing, reformers began to propose and provide for the care and training of the young. Although the ideas originated in Europe, they spread quickly to the United States where they were viewed as one solution to the problems of immigrants.

As early as 1767, Johann Friedrich Oberlin opened a creche, or day nursery, in France for the children of working parents. Although creches were soon opened in other European countries, the most well-known and most imitated early-day nurseries were those begun by the Scottish reformer Robert Owen in the early nineteenth century. Owen opened infant schools for children two years old and up in Scotland in 1816 and in New Harmony, Indiana, in 1825. In the midnineteenth century, as the idea of infant schools for the children of the poor became more widespread, Friedrich Froebel introduced the kindergarten, the *children's garden.* According to Samuel Braun and Esther Edwards, Froebel "saw and could understand what factories, life in crowded cities, the employment of parents out of the home, were doing to small children."[9] Influenced by Locke, Rousseau, and Pestalozzi, Froebel introduced ideas of respect for each child's individuality; of the importance of play as a pure, spiritual activity; and of specially designed gifts, or materials, for young children to work with. "With Froebel, modern teaching of young children becomes an entity in its own right."[10] Froebel's ideas crossed the Atlantic quickly, but for the children of the middle class rather than for the children of factory workers. Mrs. Carl Shurz opened a German-speaking kindergarten for her own children in Wisconsin in 1855. And, Elizabeth Peabody opened the first English-speaking kindergarten in the United States in Boston in 1860.

The two kinds of facilities, infant schools, or day nurseries, and kindergartens, became more common in the mid- and late-nineteenth century. By 1873, the first public kindergarten was opened in St. Louis and kindergartens began to be incorporated in public-school systems. The first facility actually called a nursery school was begun in 1908 by the MacMillan sisters in London. It offered a wide range of health, educational, nutritional, and social services to children from age one to six. Many of the early day nurseries, kindergartens, and nursery schools were philanthropic, created by well-to-do women who wanted to help the less fortunate. Like the MacMillans' school, the day nurseries offered a variety of social services. In addition, teachers trained to work in kindergartens began to bring their educational ideas to the day nurseries. They became, then, a combination of a social and educational institution. What seemed to be developing were two different trends: the full-day, multipurpose facility for the poor and the half-day, educational facility for the middle class.

By 1910, there were eighty-five nurseries serving 500 children daily in New York City. In that same year, there were 450 chapters in the Association of Day Nurseries in the United States. But the day-nursery phenomenon declined after World War I. Steinfels cites a number of reasons for that decline: the philanthropic and reform movements were less zealous; large-scale immigration stopped; there was a business recession; and, with the passage of the nineteenth amendment, feminists were less militant in their demands for the rights of women.[11] There were growing numbers of laboratory nursery schools—for the training of teachers and for the study of child development—and cooperative nursery schools—formed, administered, and sometimes taught by parents. These schools were the direct descendents of the early kindergartens and the forerunners of the part-time nursery schools of today. They were started by, and served, the middle class and omitted some of the more social-service kinds of functions of their predecessors.

There was, however, a revival of interest in the comprehensive, social-service components of early-childhood education during the Depression, when the federal government began to sponsor day-care centers. The Works Project Administration (WPA) centers were created not only to serve children but also to provide jobs for unemployed teachers and social workers. Federal aid and involvement continued during World War II, when women were needed to replace men in factories. "America," wrote Arnold Gesell and Frances Ilg in 1943, "has just allocated $6,000,000 for war nursery schools . . . nurseries created to make additional thousands of women available for war production."[12]

The end of World War II and the societal changes brought about by GI mortgages and the growth of the suburbs saw an end to federal interest in either working women or the care of young children. And then, in the late 1950s and early 1960s, three very different social and political forces created renewed interest in services for young children. Pressure for governmental involvement in the care and education of the young came from the scientific-industrial community. When the Soviet Union launched Sputnik in 1957, there were demands for better education for all children—and for that education to start as early as possible. Another source of pressure was the civil-rights movement, which sought education and care for preschool children if they were to begin school with some of the skills that more advantaged children had. Head Start, originated in the mid-1960s as a preschool remedial program for the children of poverty, was one outcome of this pressure. These pressures, in turn, led to more acceptance of nursery schools as educational rather than remedial or custodial facilities and to a proliferation of many strictly cognitive programs for the young.[13] And, finally, the women's movement began to press for universal day care to liberate women from the drudgery of the home. The idea of the all-day day nursery, of the center with comprehensive services, became, for the first time, an appealing facility for the middle class.

This somewhat hasty glimpse at a complex subject indicates that nursery schools and day-care centers do arise from similar social and educational roots. But, they have evolved in very different kinds of ways. Woolsey's distinctions are amusing but not necessarily accurate. She says that day care and nursery school provide programs that are indistinguishable. "Children build towers, mold playdough, and listen to stories in church basements."[14] She adds that when the church basement is located in the South Bronx, it is called day care; when it is located in Forest Hills, it is called nursery school. In fact most nursery schools do not offer the kinds of broad services that day-care centers do. They do not offer the hours or calendars that most working parents require. Most nursery schools are half-day programs and most operate on academic, school-year calendars. Few serve children under two years of age.

Nursery-school programs are as varied as the entire child-care system is. They provide a range of activities, usually claiming to meet the social, physical, emotional, and cognitive needs of each child. Some are affiliated with other educational institutions, such as independent schools. Some, associated with secondary schools, colleges, and universities, serve as laboratory and demonstration schools for students in education and psychology. Others perceive themselves more as play schools, as places for children to have a few hours of group experience. Philosophies range from developmental, in which the interrelated needs of each child are emphasized, to cognitive, where early number and alphabet skills are stressed. Some expect children to sit quietly for long periods of time, while others set no apparent limits on behavior. Some are connected to religious institutions, while others are parent cooperatives. Some employ highly professional, trained teachers, while others rely on community and parent volunteers.

Day care centers are varied, too. They range from private to public, from not-for-profit to profit making; they range from those that offer comprehensive services to entire families to drop-off centers with no service components.

One form of day care, often suggested as the best solution for working parents, is the employer-sponsored center. In most cases, employer-sponsored day-care centers are on-site or geographically close to a work site. This location enables parents and children to commute from home together; and it enables some parents to have an opportunity to visit or lunch with a child during the day. Corporations, hospitals, universities, and government agencies have all sponsored day-care centers. In 1978 the U.S. Department of Labor identified approximately three hundred civilian and military employer-day-care centers. In a survey of these centers, the department learned that the major benefit to employers was to better attract employees. Other benefits included lower absenteeism, improved employee attitudes, and a gain in favorable publicity. Parents' benefits included the availability of child care at low fees, the ability to have visits during the day, and the convenience of transportation. There is no mention of benefits to children.[15]

In most cases, employer-sponsored day-care centers are funded by a combination of parental fees and employer contributions. Subsidies from employers generally include in-kind services; start-up costs; and some contribution to operating expenses. Despite some notable successes,[16] in the decade between 1968 and 1978 there was actually a decrease in centers sponsored by industries and hospitals.[17] Some attribute this decrease to the fact that most families want child care close to home.[18] Others suggest causes such as high costs for both the sponsors and the employees, reduced employee demands for centers, and an adequate work force without the attraction of a day-care center.[19]

Employer-sponsored day-care centers, even when successful, present the same kinds of problems that regular day-care centers do. In contrast to nursery schools, all day-care centers must offer the long day. For that long day, both children and staff must pace themselves differently than those in the three-hour-a-day nursery school. To meet parental needs, most day-care centers do not have school vacations. The long day and the full calendar often lead to issues of high costs and low salaries; they often lead, too, to problems of burnout and boredom, fatigue and stress, for both children and adults. While many nursery-school teachers see their role as educational, many day-care-center teachers see themselves in a more comprehensive, nurturing role. Others see day-care centers and the teachers in them as fulfilling a custodial, babysitting role. While some nursery-school teachers view their jobs as part-time, supplementary, and not necessary for self-support, most day-care-center teachers do work full time and are career oriented. Therefore, day-care teachers deserve, although they do not always get, livable salaries and adequate fringe benefits.

The children in the two different kinds of settings also have differing needs. Since nursery schools generally take children at age three or four, they do not have to deal with the same kinds of separation issues that day-care centers with infants and toddlers do. In addition, the issues of health, sanitation, overstimulation, social participation, and aggression are different in each program.

Like the informal play group, however, nursery schools are not well suited to serve the needs of working parents. Those families who do use nursery schools for child care while they work must have either part-time jobs, job flexibility, and/or complex support systems to back up the nursery-school program. Working families who cannot arrange for care to supplement the nursery school cannot, therefore, rely on it as an answer to their child-care needs.

Some people suggest that the most successful kind of supplementary care is the private, in-home sitter. Approximately four-million children are cared for at home, either by relatives or nonrelatives.[20] If a capable, honest, reliable person can be employed, then this alternative seems to lead to the least stress for the child, especially for the infant and the young toddler. It solves many of the problems of continuity, of sick-child home care, of multiple caretakers, and of health risks. As the child gets older, there can be gradual transitions to play groups, nursery schools, or other part-time away-from-home programs. Unfortunately, well-trained nannies seem to be a thing of the past. People who seek this kind of employment often see it as a last resort or as a temporary measure until better employment is found. An in-home sitter is subject to many of the same stresses and demands that are placed on other child-care workers: long hours, low status, low pay, enormous responsibility. Therefore, there is apt to be a high turnover of caretakers even with this arrangement. In earlier times, career alternatives for women were so limited that childrearing was a respectable occupation for some women. Today, of course, despite continuing career limitations, women do have mobility; they have a multiple of options in business and industry; and they can get jobs with defined hours, fringe benefits, and a modicum of social status. Domestic work, never popular in our democratic society, still has a stigma attached to it. And, in most cases, in-home child care by a nonrelative is the most expensive kind of care for parents. In-home care may be the best alternative for children and for parents who can affort it; but it is not always the best solution for less-affluent parents or for adult caretakers.

Forty years ago Gesell wrote that "complex forces brought the nursery school into being. . . . The industrial revolution, economic poverty, war, urbanization, the decline of the birth rate, the progressive education movement, and the growth of the life sciences have all played a role in the establishment of day nurseries, kindergartens, preschools and child care centers."[21] He, too, made no distinction between the different kinds of programs.

In any case, the social forces that have shaped most programs have been external to the child. Like so much that deals with children's lives, programs for the care and education of young children have been most popular, have received the most public support, when the larger society has needed them: when immigrant groups needed instruction in the American way; when women had to replace men in wartime jobs; when the Soviet Union launched its first rocket ship into space; when minority groups, including women, began to seek opportunities for equal status. The growth of child-care institutions has, then, not always been based on the needs or priorities of children. Children, in many cases, have been expected to adapt to the needs of others. They receive services primarily when there are immediate consequent benefits to society at large. There is still debate about whether many of these services are in the best interests of either women or children.

13 Adult-Based Solutions

Although expansion of children's services is one solution to the problem of child care for working parents, most child-care services based on current models are not adequate. Many are problematic for both children and adults. Most were designed with children's needs subordinate to adult needs and with women's needs subordinate to men's needs. Therefore, it is important to look at other kinds of proposals, proposals that rely more on adult solutions than child solutions. All solutions should, of course, take into account the requirements of all of the constituencies involved, including women and children.

One common adult-based proposal, often seen as a panacea, is for the expansion of information and referral services.[1] These agencies, called more familiarly I&Rs, are both public and private, and help clarify the various options available to parents. I&Rs keep track of openings and spaces in many different kinds of child-care programs. To apply the words of industry to the lives of children, I&Rs monitor supply and demand; they serve the consumers of child-care services. Although I&Rs usually cannot evaluate individual programs, many do maintain records of parental satisfaction or complaint. The impetus for these services and for their expansion seems to reflect a lack of knowledge, a naïveté, on the part of many parents about different kinds of child care. For some parents, I&Rs are the only alternative to the Yellow Pages for the location of child-care programs. This sad situation exists both because of the mobility and isolation of so many families and also because most people growing up in the United States learn a great deal about cars, about computers, about sports heroes but little about children and their needs. They learn even less about the services required to meet those needs. In any case, the success of I&Rs depends on adequate, affordable child-care services. I&Rs can help parents find solutions, perhaps, but I&Rs are hardly a solution themselves.

Some people have suggested that eventually technology will provide a solution for child care. Large numbers of people will be able to work at home at their computer terminals and take care of their children while they work. A study by the Institute for the Future predicts that 40 percent of U.S. households will have videotex terminals by the year 1998. These systems will change current patterns of employment, shopping, schooling, and family life.[2] In fact, the New York Telephone Company is already experimenting with a home office of the future, called the *business marketing work-at-home project.* One couple has been able to take care of their ten-month-old child by working at home on alternate days in what is called an *electronic cottage.* Despite the success of this experiment, both parents admit that they would not want to spend all of their working time at home. And, the article describing the experiment does not mention what the parents do when the child's needs interfere with work demands. But the article does say that the parents understand that, as the child gets older, they will need supplementary help,[3] for, of course, child care is work. It is difficult, even impossible, to sit at a computer terminal and communicate with colleagues and carry out professional responsibilities while caring for a child. Anyone who endorses this technological solution devalues the job, devalues the child, and devalues the work of childrearing.

Perhaps the most common suggestion for an adult-based solution to child-care problems is composed of several possible changes in work policies. All changes require a different work model than the current one, which Alice Rossi refers to as one of "great emphasis on work and little emphasis on family."[4] Other policy analysts, too, advise the restructuring of the work model:

> A basic change in the work-role model may be necessary for both men and women. The male work-role model in our society calls for full-time, continuous work from graduation to retirement, subordination of other roles to work, and actualization of one's potential through it. To a large extent, men could give work this emphasis because women supported the male work role, subordinated their own work role, and carried out most of the family role. In the past, with some stress, one breadwinner in the family could follow the male work model. In the present, with more stress, one breadwinner could emphasize work and another breadwinner play an ancillary, less demanding work role. But it is doubtful whether large numbers of families can function with both partners following the male work model. For both spouses to adopt the male work model, families would have to stop having children, or else household and childcare services would have to be provided on a scale hitherto unprecedented. Without one or the other, two-role living by both men and women will require a new work-role model and for men an expanded family role.[5]

Work-model alternatives include flex-time and part-time work; extended maternity and paternity benefits; and reassurances about job security without penalty after child-care leaves-of-absence.

The flexible-working-hour model, or flex-time, seems to solve not only many of the problems of preschool child care but also of after-school care for older children. In 1978 President Carter signed a flex-time bill that authorized experimental programs in executive and military departments. The programs were designed to solve a variety of issues, including child care, mass transit, and energy consumption. In 1981, the *Congressional Quarterly* reported that between 2.5 and 3.5 million people were participating in flex-time programs. Employers reported improved productivity and declines in absences and lateness. As predicted, people elected flex-time for a variety of reasons. But a study of 700 flex-time government employees found that the majority of those participating for family reasons were women.[6] Thus, the alternative work model is seen as a solution for family problems for women but not for men. As usual, when it comes to changes for family reasons, it is the women who are making the compromises.

Another popular suggested work-model change is for the expansion of part-time work with guarantees of job status, seniority, and full fringe benefits.[7] Among the benefits recommended are "paid personal days specifically for children and family, and paid disability and personal leaves for more than six weeks for pregnancy and maternity."[8] In some cases, the suggestion is for so-called cafeteria-style benefits. This concept enables parents to choose from a variety of fringe-benefit options. In other words, parents could give up something like dental insurance or tuition reimbursement for more personal days for the care of a sick child. Most of the proposals for changes in fringe-benefit options are, however, merely proposals and are not being implemented to any degree. For instance, in a 1980 survey by Catalyst of over three hundred major corporations, less than 8 percent had cafeteria fringe benefits.[9] The one hopeful sign for the future is that over 60 percent of the corporations responding were in favor of the practice.

In the General Mills Study, *Families at Work*, a majority of women preferred part-time to full-time work. In fact, more than half of the women interviewed who held executive, managerial, or professional positions expressed preferences for part-time work.[10] In its survey of human-resource officers, the General Mills study found that two-thirds expected their companies to adopt job-sharing policies; and a majority expected that their companies would seek more flexible work schedules. Interestingly, the authors of the study preface this finding as being "of special importance to women planning to work."[11] Once again it seems to be women and not men for whom part-time alternatives are designed; it is the women who are making the compromises.

Some people advocate the extension of maternity and paternity leaves as a solution for the child-care problem. According to the Pregnancy Discrimination Act of 1978, pregnancy and childbirth are treated as disabilities. Therefore, employers are legally required to provide the same kinds of leaves as they do for other illnesses. In most cases, this leave is six-to-eight weeks.[12] Beyond that legal requirement, there is a wide range of employer policies. In a 1980 survey by the New York Chamber of Commerce and Industry, companies reported on how long they would keep a job open while an employee took maternity leave. The time spans reported ranged from eight weeks to six months. In fact, 11 percent of the companies replied that they would hold a job indefinitely. But 21 percent admitted that they would not keep the job open at all.[13]

There is variation, too, in employer policies for paternal leaves. Although more and more companies are adopting policies for paternal leaves that are similar to their maternal-leave policies,[14] there are still companies that deny leaves to men and that will not assure fathers of either their jobs or their seniority.[15] Even if many employers do institute policies for paternal child-care leave, it is not certain that large numbers of fathers will avail themselves of the option. In Sweden, in the years from 1974 to 1979, only 15 percent of eligible fathers took advantage of a paternal-leave policy that guarantees 90 percent of regular salary and reemployment without loss of seniority.[16] Whether or not companies offer—or fathers utilize—paternal leaves, these leaves are, after all, for rather brief periods of time. Even an extended leave similar to Sweden's is only for nine months and hardly solves the issues of long-term child care for working parents.

Another solution proposed by various experts, which involves more participation by fathers, is the partnership—the idea of shared care.[17] As Daniels and Weingarten point out, "It used to be that a woman's entire adult life might be consumed in the bearing and rearing of children. Today, a family of two spaced two or three years apart means full-time parenthood—in the sense of daily absorption in the care of totally dependent children—for nine years at most, from the birth of the first until the second enters first grade. This is only *one-sixth* of a hypothetical adult life span of 54 years, from age 21 to 75 (italics in original)."[18] Daniels and Weingarten add that for men and women both, the awareness of parenting as a brief segment in the entire life cycle should permit them to plan for the other five-sixths of that adult life. "Child bearing and child rearing are not, any more, a continuous undercurrent of adult existence, but rather a circumscribed period of years (when) men and women can participate jointly in the care of their young children."[19]

There are problems with shared care, also. In a study by Graeme Russell of fifty Australian families in which fathers had equal or greater childrearing roles than mothers, mothers still complained about physical demands, especially "the rush and exhaustion"; and they felt guilty leaving children even with their fathers. On the other hand, fathers complained about "the constant demands of the caregiving role and the criticisms of their male peer group."[20] There were, of course, trade-offs. While women felt more independent, more satisfied with themselves and their jobs, and fathers felt improved relationships with their children, husbands and wives spent less time together and reported more tension between them. In fact, two years after the first study, Russell studied eighteen of the original fifty families and found that half had adopted a traditional life style for their families.

In any case, it seems unlikely that there will be a burst of enthusiasm for shared care of children as long as there are gross inequalities in men's and women's earning power. If women earn 60 percent of what men earn, if professional women earn salaries equivalent to less skilled men, then raising children will continue to be women's work. It may be interesting to speculate about shared care, about equal partnerships, about the joys of fathering. But as long as men command the higher salaries, and gain the most job status, and have the best chances for advancement, and remain in positions of power, then, in most cases, women will make the trade-offs necessary to raise the children. Despite many recent changes in our society, and sometimes because of these recent changes, women are still in a no-win situation.

It is too soon to detemine what effects any of these work-model changes might have on children. But, there is another trend that will have serious impact on their lives—and that is the adoption by some women of what Rossi calls the "male pattern" of parenting. "Men turn their fathering on and off" for their own personal convenience or to suit their business schedules. They view parenting "from a distance, as an appendage to, or consequence of, mating, rather than the focus of family systems and individual lives."[21]

It is, perhaps, this imitation by women of the traditional male pattern of relating to children that has led to the dehumanization of childhood, to the treatment of children as things. It has enabled parents to leave infants and young children with questionable caretakers in questionable surroundings. It has encouraged parents to seek out bargain substitutes to nurture and teach their young. It has stressed a narcissism that places personal fulfillment above all other human endeavors and human relationships. It has permitted parents to consider natural childbirth and a three-week-new-baby-leave-of-absence as their major responsibility for bonding and for attachment. It has created a generation of young children whose illnesses are either ignored or minimized so that they are rarely free of debilitating, often contagious, symptoms. It has justified what frequently amounts to neglect by endorsing the elusive, even fictional, quality time.

To call this male pattern of relating to children parenting is to admire the Emperor's clothes.[22] Just as the Emperor's new clothes were nonexistent, so too is parenting nonexistent when both parents adopt the traditional male pattern of relating to children.

Adult-based solutions for child care for working parents reflect changes in work-role models and in family-role models. Changes in the work-role model are really changes for and at the expense of women. Changes in the family-role model, in which women adopt traditionally male patterns but men do not adopt traditionally female patterns, are clearly at the expense of children. Once again, it is women and children who must bear the burdens of change.

14 Rethinking Our Priorities

There are no easy answers, no quick fixes, no victimless solutions to the problems of child care for working parents. Those who make claims for easy answers are deceiving both themselves and the public. They demean child development as well as child care. They minimize the role of the family in a civilized society. They overlook the historical fact that in times of transition or stress, it is women and children who have been the first to make the trade-offs and the compromises.

There are, and always have been, children who are resilient and strong. They adjust to unusual life stresses and seem to emerge healthy, both physically and psychologically. There are, and always have been, women who can successfully cope with all of the conflicts of career and family. Although they are often referred to as superwomen, there is nothing magical about their success. They are exceptionally hard working; they are exceptionally competent. Finally, there are, and probably always will be, gifted, intelligent teachers who are able to remain in day-care centers and nurture children without suffering from feelings of exploitation and burnout.

But, there are, and always will be, children and women who are not so strong and resilient. For them, perhaps for the large majority, our society must create viable alternatives for careers and for child care. Yet, alternatives will become real only when society rethinks its priorities: when men and women are truly equals; when child-based solutions are based on the needs of children; when adult-based solutions consider the needs of women; and when parents acknowledge that they have a responsibility to raise their children. Having a child is not the same as buying a chair or acquiring a pet. Having a child involves a physical, moral, intellectual, emotional, and financial commitment to take care of that child. Taking care of a child often entails personal and professional trade-offs, even sacrifices. But all of these trade-offs and sacrifices would be less severe if both parents, as equal partners, made them. Together, parents must assume the task of childrearing and they must do so diligently and conscientiously.

Amitai Etzioni has written that "in any other industry, if you remove a million employees without reducing the job requirements very much, nobody would deny that the industry is woefully shorthanded. If we take a million women out of a million households to work outside the home, and replace them with precious little in child-care services, few babysitters, and little more grandparenting, then the parenting 'industry' is woefully shorthanded. . . . This is not an argument for women to stay home to do the parenting, but for *someone* to do more of it (italics in original)."[1]

It *is* necessary for someone to raise the children and raising children is work. Whether it is done by a mother, by a father, by a relative, by a family-day-care provider, by an at-home sitter, by a day-care center, or by a combination of the above, it is work. It can be boring, frustrating, lonely, fatiguing, thankless, repetitive, claustrophobic. But it can also be warm, stimulating, satisfying, challenging, joyful, fleeting. Society must redefine and reevaluate childrearing so that it is not considered demeaning and worthless work but important work. As Kenneth Keniston points out, "child rearing, despite its pleasures and rewards, is a real job, perhaps the most important one for a vigorous society, but it does not provide a salary when carried out by parents, yields no pension rights, and is not even counted in the GNP."[2]

It is a real job and a most important one. If a man and a woman desire to have children, they must decide how they are going to raise them and how they are going to pay for the raising of them. If they cannot afford—or do not want—to give up some career time to raise their children, then they must be selective. They must be prepared to value and respect the person or persons whom they employ to do that work for them. Those persons deserve social approval and monetary rewards that reflect the enormity of their task. If parents want to have two careers and children, they should investigate child-care options *before* they conceive. They should advertise for sitters or housekeepers and should interview some to see if there are suitable people available at a price they can afford. They should visit family-day-care homes and group-day-care centers and should spend *at least* two full days at each place. They should then decide whether any of those places are environments where they themselves could spend ten hours a day, fifty hours a week. Both mother and father should determine the sick-child policy for their particular family. If either parent has a position where much of the work can be done at home and where there is enough flexibility for emergencies, then they have a relatively easy solution. However, if both careers are rigid, then they must explore options for the care of sick children as well as routine care. Only when a dual-career couple has determined that there are in fact suitable alternatives for the care and raising of children should they have them.

If couples claim that they cannot afford to live on one salary, they should rethink their priorities. No one wants to reduce economic or social status, but sometimes it is necessary. And, in a field that talks consistently about trade-offs, parents should be able to make a few. They should be able to decide that for a few years they might have to sacrifice, but they will do it for their family. Actually, as evident in earlier chapters, if day-care centers and family-day-care providers charged what they were worth, or if they gave the kind of quality environment children deserve, child care would be every bit as costly as one parent not working. Further, as women who work in day care gain more power, perhaps the standards for day-care salaries will increase and day care will not be such a bargain. In that event, most couples will *have* to give more thought to reproducing.

When couples do reproduce, they should do so with what Erikson calls *generativity*, "the concern in establishing and guiding the next generation." Erikson points out that wanting or having children does not automatically entail generativity. He speaks of some individuals who "do not apply this drive to their own offspring." "In fact," he says, "some young parents suffer, it seems, from the retardation of the ability to develop this stage. The reasons are often to be found in early childhood impressions; in excessive self-love based on a too strenuously self-made personality; and finally . . . in the lack of some faith, some 'belief in the species,' which would make a child appear to be a welcome trust of the community."[3]

If children are to be *a welcome trust of the community*, then child-care options must be designed with the needs and demands of the child as central. But, these options cannot be at the expense of caretakers. Children are entitled to a healthy, secure, consistent, loving, disciplined, warm, caring, nurtured, unpressured infancy and childhood. It is primarily the responsibility of parents to so provide. But, it is the responsibility of the greater society to create structures and policies that enable parents to do so. These structures and policies must be attractive, viable, and equitable for both men and women. They must be as beneficial or as sacrificial for men as they are for women. They must enable men—physically, economically, psychologically, socially—to accept their generativity, their responsibility for guiding the next generation.

New structures must mean that society ends the vicious circle in which men earn more money and have more status than women. Because women earn less, they are the ones to leave their jobs; they are the ones to experiment with alternative work models. Because of salary discrepancies, women—mothers, day-care teachers, family-day-care providers, in-home sitters—are left, almost by default, to raise the children. Because the salaries and the esteem women get for raising children are so demeaning, few men will consider it seriously. If women's outide income were competitive with men's, if raising children paid better, and if it were considered admirable, then, perhaps, more men would get involved in childrearing both as fathers and as caregivers. This involvement, no doubt, would lead to improvements in both salary and status for *all* caregivers, male and female, parent and professional. New structures might include, but must improve upon, the old suggestions. Center-based care could be an option, but it would have to be funded adequately. Center-based care could be used with satellite family-day-care systems so that children might have a group experience for part of the day and a home experience for the other part. All center-based care should have enough trained personnel, and enough status and salary for that personnel, so that men might select it as a career option; so that no one would feel exploited; so that teachers could experience exhilaration about working with children; so that consistency rather than turnover would become the labor pattern. Center-based care should have adequate space and personnel for some form of infirmary. But, it should also have consulting sick-child home-health people whom the children actually *know* and who are available for home health care when necessary. Center-based care should have sufficient space so that children are not crowded—not forced to eat and sleep and play, and even toilet—in the same space.

Family-day-care homes should not be isolated and should not be exploitative of the providers. All providers should receive wages equal to their tasks. And, in recognition of the importance of child care and the stresses of it, perhaps family-day-care pairings could be explored. Several women—or, in an equal world, several men, or one or two of each—could share the responsibilities for a small number of children. With a reasonable adult-child ratio, with adequate salaries, with rotating schedules, and with sufficient supervision and consultation, neither providers nor children would be too overwhelmed. All participants, in fact, might flourish from the experience. There could be a new kind of domestic peace corps available for child care for those families who must have supplementary help. After all, there should be as much respect given to people who help raise the next generation as is given to those who help underdeveloped foreign societies.

For parents who choose to raise their children themselves, there should be rewards not penalties. In fact, if our society really valued its children and childrearing, then parents could receive something similar to the GI Bill of Rights—if one parent chooses to take time off to raise a child, or if parents wish to share in that effort, they could get some reassurances about resumption of employment without total loss of seniority. There could be mechanisms within our employment and social-security systems so that those who do stay home to raise the children are considered employed, are accepted as contributing to the greater good of the entire community.

Employers might offer more flexibility in terms of hours, work weeks, and fringe benefits. There might be options for sick-child care, for extended maternity and paternity leaves, for the care of children during school vacations. And, all of these options should be available and used by both fathers and mothers. With true equality in the job market, with sensitive men and women in positions of power, there might be changes in the adult-work model that give consideration to family needs, to human needs.

In a 1965 edition of Roget's Thesaurus, the phrase *women and children* is listed under the heading *hindrance* and the subcategory *encumbrance*.[4] There is the entry, at number 702, on page 426: *women and children*, immediately after *white elephant* and immediately preceding *passenger; mortgage, debts*. Of course, a thesaurus does not create or even reflect public policy. But, it does sometimes reflect attitudes, and many generations have apparently perceived women and children as an encumbrance, as a white elephant. It is time for such attitudes to stop.

Society must rethink its priorities. If children are as important as offshore oil; if they are as interesting as computers; if they are as vital to the survival of the United States as nuclear missiles; if they are a national treasure equal to the Grand Canyon; then *someone will have to raise them*. And, someone—including parents and the larger society—will have to pay for that care. Children should be a welcome trust of the community. Neither children nor women should be considered an encumbrance. Nor, should they need to be first. Instead, men and women and children need to be first together, sharing a common humanity, a common interest in the future.

Appendix

Table A-1
Child-Development Chart

Approximate Age	*Cognitive Theory Piaget*	*Psychosocial Theory Erikson*	*Psychosexual Theory Freud*
Birth to Twelve months	*Early sensorimotor stage* Moves from reflexive behavior to intentional activities Conscious only of the present, the tangible, the here and now: out of sight, out of mind	*Trust versus mistrust* Totally dependent on caretakers for feeding, for continuity, and for consistency of care Builds basic trust through satisfaction by adults of infantile demands Develops confidence in environment, in the future	*Oral stage* Dominated by the id, by instincts Preoccupied with immediate gratification of impulses Derives pleasure from mouth: sucking and biting
Twelve months to Twenty-four months	*Late sensorimotor stage* Begins to develop object permanence: can be conscious of an absent, unseen person or thing Thinks in primitive, rudimentary manner Begins awareness of time and space	*Autonomy versus shame, doubt* Begins to explore, manipulate, discriminate Exercises choice, self-restraint Develops sense of self-control, of pride in own accomplishments, of optimism, good will Adjusts to external, social demands, but must develop and retain sense of competence, of autonomy	*Early anal stage* Begins to develop ego, sense of self Derives pleasure from expulsion and retention of feces
Twenty-four months to Sixty months	*Preoperational stage* Begins to acquire symbolic representation: mental images, labels, memory Sees things egocentrically from own point of view Lets perception dominate reason: believes what can be seen Solves problems intuitively, not logically, but begins to test for cause and effect Begins skill development Derives satisfaction from the development and mastery of new skills	*Initiative versus guilt* Begins to form goals, ambitions, ideals Gradually develops sense of right and wrong, of moral responsibility Because of the trust experienced and the autonomy acquired, enters new situations with self-confidence, idealism, initiative	*Late anal stage* Develops muscular control *Oedipal stage* Resolves Oedipal and Electra conflicts: moves from desire for opposite-sex parent to identification with same-sex parent and to desire for outside love object Accepts appropriate age and sex roles Develops superego, or conscience Derives pleasure from genital stimulation

Table A-2
Some Examples of the Research

Researchers	*Number of Subjects*	*Ages*	*Socio-Economic Status*	*Kind of Care*	*Method*	*Major Findings*	*Source*
Anderson et al.	35	preschool	middleclass	group-day-care centers	Strange Situation, adapted to assess relationships with caregivers	Children showed more indications of secure attachment to highly involved caregivers than they did to less involved caregivers.	*Child Development* (1981) 52.1:53-61
Baumrind and Black	103	mean age: forty-seven months	middleclass	university day-care center	naturalistic observations	Certain parental behaviors (allowing independence, interacting verbally, enforcing demands, disciplining consistently) were associated with competent, stable, assertive preschoolers.	*Child Development* (1967) 38:291-327
Blanchard and Main	21	one to two years	middleclass	day care approximately thirty-nine hours per week twelve months per year	Strange Situation	The longer the period of time children spent in day care, the less evidence they showed of social-emotional maladjustments.	*Developmental Psychology* (1979) 15:445-446
Blehar	40	two and three years	middleclass	twenty home reared, twenty in full-time daycare	Strange Situation	Mother-child relationships appeared disturbed by child's attendance in day care.	*Child Development* (1974) 45:683-692
Bradley and Caldwell	77	six months and re-tested at three years	—	home reared	family observed and interviewed; Bayley Scales of Infant Development at six months. Stanford Binet Intelligence Scale at three years.	Kind of stimulation in home environment affects the cognitive development of the child.	*Developmental Psychology* (1976) 12:93-97

Brookhart and Hock	23	ten to twelve months	middleclass	fifteen day care; eight home care	Strange Situation	No discernible effects based on type of rearing were found.	*Child Development* (1976) 47:333-340
Caldwell et al.	41	approximately thirty months	lowerclass	eighteen day care; twenty-three home care	observations, interviews, developmental testing	No differences in attachment patterns could be found between the two groups.	*American Journal of Orthopsychiatry* (1970) 40:397-412
Charlesworth and Hartup	70	three to four years	middleclass	laboratory preschool	naturalistic observations	Older peers give more positive reinforcement for social behavior than younger children.	*Child Development* (1967) 38:993-1002
Cochran	120	twelve, fifteen, and eighteen months	—	sixty in day-care centers; thirty-four, at home with mothers; twenty-six, home with family-day-care mother	naturalistic observations of separations; also comparisons of mental development and attachment	No overall differences on an infant scale or in a separation situation were found, although home-care children explored their surroundings and interacted more in cognitive-verbal situations than day-care children.	*Child Development* (1977) 48.1:702-707
Cornelius and Denny	64	four to five years	middleclass	thirty-two day care; thirty-two home care	Strange Situation, with mothers and with other adults	No differences were found between home-raised and center-raised children, except that home-reared girls sought proximity to mothers more than home-reared boys.	*Developmental Psychology* (1975) 11:575-582
Doyle	24	five to thirty months	—	twelve day care; twelve home care	Strange Situation in a laboratory and in a home setting	No evidence of weak or insecure attachments was found.	*Developmental Psychology* (1975) 11:655-656
Farran and Ramey	23	nine to thirty-one months	lowerclass	day care	mildly stressful situation that forced choice among attachment figures, mothers or caregivers	Infants preferred proximity to and interactions with mothers.	*Child Development* (1977) 48.2:1112-1116
Fox	122	eight to twenty-four months	—	kibbutz	Strange Situation	Mother and caregiver apparently were interchangeable attachment figures.	*Child Development* (1977) 48.2:1228-1239

Table A-2 *(continued)*

Researchers	*Number of Subjects*	*Ages*	*Socio-Economic Status*	*Kind of Care*	*Method*	*Major Findings*	*Source*
Kohen-Raz	361	one to twenty-seven months	middleclass	home-reared; kibbutz reared; institution reared	Bayley Mental and Motor Scales	Kibbutz and home-reared children scored equally on mental and motor scales and scored higher than institutionalized children.	*Child Development* (1968) 39:489-504
Macrae and Herbert-Jackson	16	twenty-four months	mixed	day care	center caregivers' ratings	Findings suggest different effects from different programs; observations about one day-care center do not necessarily apply to all day-care centers.	*Developmental Psychology* (1976) 12:269-270
McCutcheon and Calhoun	19	five to thirty months	middleclass	day care	naturalistic observations for social and emotional adjustment	A decrease of crying, remaining alone, and interacting with adults was found and corresponding increase of interactions with peers as children adjusted to the day-care setting.	*American Journal of Orthopsychiatry* (1976) 46:104-108
Moskowitz et al.	24	approximately forty-two months	—	twelve, six months of day-care experience; twelve, no group experience	Strange Situation modification	Few differences were found between the groups; but there was some suggestion that day-care children were less upset when stressed and less interested in a strange adult; study found no group differences in behaviors toward mothers.	*Child Development* (1977) 48.2:1271-1276
Portnoy and and Simmons	35	three and one-half to four years	middleclass	Group 1: home care with mothers Group 2: home with mothers until three, then in day care	Strange Situation modification	No significant differences in attachment patterns were found in children with different childrearing histories.	*Child Development* (1978) 49:239-242

				Group 3: family day care at one, then group care at approximately three			
Ragozin	34	seventeen to thirty-eight months	middleclass	twenty day care; fourteen home care	naturalistic observations and Strange Situation	Preference for mother over caregiver was found; day-care group interacted less with stranger; day care seemed compatible with normal attachment behaviors.	*Child Development* (1980) 51:409-415
Raph et al.	97	three to five years	—	children with no nursery-school experience compared to children with nursery-school experience	naturalistic observations	Age of entrance to preschool and length of that attendance influence the frequency of children's interactions with peers and with teachers in kindergarten; those children who had been in school longest had fewer negative interactions with peers and more negative interactions with teachers.	*American Journal of Orthopsychiatry* (1968) 38:144-152
Robinson and Robinson	31	infants to four and one-half years	mixed	day care	Bayley Mental and Motor Scales; Bayley Behavior Profile; variety of standardized tests	High-quality group care had positive effect on verbal skills; effects were greater with deprived than with more advantaged.	*Child Development* (1971) 42:1673-1683
Rubenstein et al.	65	five to six months	lowerclass	thirty-eight mother-reared; fifteen care with relatives; twelve care with nonrelatives	naturalistic observations	No noticeable differences were found between children with mothers or with substitute caregivers.	*Developmental Psychology* (1977) 13:529-530

Table A-2 *(continued)*

Researchers	*Number of Subjects*	*Ages*	*Socio-Economic Status*	*Kind of Care*	*Method*	*Major Findings*	*Source*
Rubenstein and Howes	30	seventeen to twenty months	middleclass	fifteen day care; fifteen home care	naturalistic observations	Day care had no adverse effects in social and play behavior; peers were important social objects for toddlers and helped ease separation from adult caregivers.	*Developmental Psychology* (1979) 15:1-24
Schwarz et al.	40	forty-two and forty-six months	—	twenty in day care since five to twenty-two months; twenty at home until three years	naturalistic observations	No evidence was found to indicate that group that entered day care as infants showed greater emotional insecurity.	*American Journal of Orthopsychiatry* (1973) 43:340-346
Schwarz et al.	38	three to four years	lower and middleclass	nineteen with day care; nineteen without day care	observations and teacher ratings	The day-care group was more aggressive, more emotionally active, and less cooperative with adults.	*Developmental Psychology* (1974) 10:502-506
Winett et al.	124	three to five and one-half years	middleclass	four groups: one group, all-day day care; one group, all day with babysitter; one group, mixed center and sitter; one group, home care	various standardized tests	Day-care and home-care groups did not differ significantly on child measures, although the mixed group scored highest on measures of intellectual ability.	*Journal of Community Psychology* (1977) 5:149-159

Endnotes

Chapter 1

1. Sheila B. Kamerman, *Parenting in an Unresponsive Society*, pp. 8-13; U.S. Department of Labor, *Twenty Facts on Women Workers* (Washington, D.C.: Office of the Secretary, Women's Bureau, 1980).

2. Edward F. Zigler and Pauline Turner, "Parents and Day Care Workers: A Failed Partnership?," in Edward Zigler and Edmund Gordon, eds., *Day Care*, p. 175.

3. See David Elkind, *The Hurried Child.*

4. *Christian Science Monitor*, 4 October 1982.

5. Ibid., 27 September 1982.

6. Edward M. Kennedy, "Child Care—A Commitment to be Honored," in Zigler and Gordon, eds., *Day Care*, p. 261.

7. See Deborah Fallows, "What Day Care Can't Do," *Newsweek*, 10 January 1983; Selma Fraiberg, *Every Child's Birthright*; Beatrice Glickman and Nesha Springer, *Who Cares for the Baby?*; Elizabeth Jones and Elizabeth Prescott, "Day Care: Short- or Long-Term Solution?," in the Annals, American Academy of Political and Social Science, *Young Children and Social Policy*, pp. 91-101; Paul D. Meier and Linda Burnett, *The Unwanted Generation* (Grand Rapids: Baker Book House, 1980); Burton White, "Should You Stay Home with Your Baby?," *Young Children* 36 (November 1981):11-17; Suzanne Woolsey, "Pied Piper Politics and the Child-Care Debate."

8. Sally Provence, Audrey Naylor, and June Patterson, *The Challenge of Daycare*, p. 1.

9. Elizabeth Hagen, "Child Care and Women's Liberation," in Roby, ed., *Child Care—Who Cares?*, p. 117.

10. Margaret Steinfels, *Who's Minding the Children?*, p. 13.

11. Dominique Browning, "Waiting for Mommy," *Texas Monthly*, February 1982, p. 193.

12. W. Gary Winget, "The Dilemma of Affordable Child Care," in Zigler and Gordon, eds., *Day Care*, pp. 351-352.

13. Alison Clarke-Stewart, *Day Care*, p. 136.

14. Valerie Suransky, *The Erosion of Childhood*, p. 185.

15. Edward Zigler and Jody Goodman, " The Battle for Day Care in America: A View from the Trenches," in Zigler and Gordon, eds., *Day Care*, p. 340.

Chapter 2

1. *New York Times*, 1 July 1982.
2. U.S. Department of Labor, *Twenty Facts on Women Workers* (Washington, D.C.: Office of the Secretary, Women's Bureau, 1980).
3. Sheila B. Kamerman, *Parenting in an Unresponsive Society*, p. 11.
4. U.S. Department of Labor, *Twenty Facts*.
5. Edward Zigler and Jody Goodman, "The Battle for Day Care in America: A View from the Trenches," in Zigler and Gordon, eds., *Day Care*, p. 338.
6. *New York Times*, 24 May 1982, p. B5.
7. David Elkind, *The Hurried Child*, p. 38.
8. Pamela Daniels and Kathy Weingarten, *Sooner or Later*, p. 5.
9. *New York Times*, 28 May 1982.
10. Daniels and Weingarten, *Sooner or Later*, p. 327.
11. Jane Price, *You're Not Too Old to Have a Baby*, p. 60.
12. Daniels and Weingarten, *Sooner or Later*, p. 193.
13. J. Stene et al., "Paternal Age and Down's Syndrome," *Human Genetics* 59 (1981):119-124.
14. U.S. Department of Health and Human Services, *Amniocentesis for Prenatal Chromosomal Diagnosis*, p. 15.
15. *New York Times*, 16 February 1982, p. C1.
16. M.M. Kappelman and P.R. Ackerman, *Parents After Thirty*, p. 65.
17. Daniels and Weingarten, *Sooner or Later*, p. 185.
18. See Florence Howe, "Sexual Stereotypes Start Early," *Saturday Review*, 16 October 1971; Ailleen Nilsen, "Women in Children's Literature," *College English*, May 1971.
19. See Elkind, *The Hurried Child*.
20. *Boston Globe*, 17 November 1982, p. 68.
21. *Miami Herald*, 30 October 1982, p. 1 BR.
22. Personal Communication, Ellen Blumenthal, M.D.
23. *New York Times*, 21 October 1982, p. A20.
24. *American Psychological Association Monitor*, October 1982.
25. *New York Times*, 12 April 1982.
26. Ibid., 10 January 1982.
27. Constructive Playthings Catalogue (Leawood, Kans.: Constructive Playthings, 1982-1983), p. 49. Reprinted with permission.
28. Community Playthings Catalogue (Rifton, N.Y.: Community Playthings, 1982), p. 2. Reprinted with permission.
29. Alfax Furniture Catalogue (New York: Alfax Manufacturing Co.), p. 10. Reprinted with permission. Please note: Alfax has discontinued advertising and distributing this product.

30. Hertz Furniture Systems Catalogue (New York: Hertz Furniture Systems Co.), p. 16. Reprinted with permission.

31. *New York Times*, 2 September 1983, p. C3.

32. Childcraft Catalogue, *The Growing Years* (Edison, N.J.: Childcraft Education Corp., 1982-1983), p. 16. Reprinted with permission.

33. Hertz Catalogue, p. 16.

34. Ibid., p. 16.

35. Continental Plastic Card Co., Flyer (Coral Springs, Fla.). Reprinted with permission.

36. Dorothy Cohen, "Help the Child to Become Human," *Young Children* 34 (November 1979):2.

Chapter 3

1. Richard Ruopp et al., *Children at the Center*.

2. Mary D. Keyserling, *Windows on Day Care*.

3. Erik H. Erikson, *Childhood and Society*, pp. 247-251.

4. Jean Piaget, *The Construction of Reality in the Child*, pp. 3-96.

5. Selma Fraiberg, *The Magic Years*.

6. John Bowlby, "The Nature of the Child's Tie to His Mother," *International Journal of Psychoanalysis* 39 (1958):350-373; Bowlby, "Separation Anxiety," *International Journal of Psychoanalysis* 41 (1960):89-113; Rene Spitz, "Hospitalism: An Inquiry into the Genesis of Psychiatric Conditioning in Early Childhood," in Feneschel et al., *Psychoanalytic Study of the Child* 1 (New York: International Universities Press, 1945), pp. 53-74.

7. Howard Gardner, *Developmental Psychology*, p. 37.

8. Mary Ainsworth, *Infancy in Uganda* (Baltimore: Johns Hopkins University Press, 1967); B.M. Lester et al., "Separation Protest in Guatemalan Infants: Cross-Cultural and Cognitive Findings," *Developmental Psychology* 10 (1974):79-85; S. Provence and R.C. Lipton, *Infants in Institutions* (New York: International Universities Press, 1963).

9. Michael Rutter, "Parent-Child Separation: Psychological Effects on the Children," *Journal of Child Psychology and Psychiatry* 12 (1971): 233-260; H. Rheingold and C.O. Eckerman, "Fear of the Stranger: A Critical Examination," in H. Reese, ed., *Advances in Child Development and Behavior* 7 (New York: Academic Press, 1973); see also B. Glickman and N. Springer, *Who Cares for the Baby?*, pp. 162-193 for the report of an interview with Jerome Kagan.

10. Nina R. Lief, *The First Year of Life* (Los Angeles: Sadlier, 1982), p. 22.

11. B. Wilcox et al., "A Comparison of Individual and Multiple Assignment of Caregivers to Infants in Day Care," *Merrill-Palmer Quarterly* 25:53-62.

12. Marcy Whitebook et al., "Who's Minding the Child Care Workers?," p. 2.

13. Edward Zigler and Edmund Gordon, eds., *Day Care*, p. 497.

14. S. Cornelius and N. Denney, "Dependency in Day Care and Home Care Children," *Developmental Psychology* 11 (1975):575-582; A. Doyle, "Infant Development in Day Care," *Developmental Psychology* 11 (1975): 655-656.

15. U.S. Department of Health, Education, and Welfare, *The Appropriateness of the Federal Interagency Day Care Requirements*, p. 61.

16. There is almost a lilting tone to the copy for a diaper pail in a catalog of equipment and supplies for preschoolers: "This jumbo 30 quart capacity pail is made of sturdy white plastic and has molded-in handles and a sealed cover that has a giant sized holder for all kinds of solid deodorants." Constructive Playthings Catalogue (Leawood, Kans.: 1982-1983), p. 49. Reprinted with permission.

17. Ruopp et al., *Children at the Center*, pp. 140-149.

18. Commonwealth of Massachusetts, Filing and Publication Regulations 102, p. 168.

19. Esphyr Slobodkina, *Caps for Sale* (New York: W.R. Scott, 1949).

20. U.S. Department of Health, Education, and Welfare, *The Appropriateness of FIDCR*, p. 61.

21. Jay Belsky, Laurence Steinberg, and Ann Walker, "The Ecology of Day Care," in Michael Lamb, ed., *Nontraditional Families*, p. 106.

22. Anna Freud, "The Emotional and Social Development of Young Children," in Belan Mills, ed., *Understanding the Young Child and His Curriculum*, p. 69.

23. Valerie Suransky, *The Erosion of Childhood*, p. 188.

Chapter 5

1. Richard Ruopp and Jeffrey Travers, "Janus Faces Day Care: Perspectives on Quality and Cost," in Zigler and Gordon, eds., *Day Care*, pp. 88-89.

2. Marcy Whitebook et al., "Who's Minding the Child Care Workers?," p. 2.

3. *Working Mother*, October 1982, p. 126.

4. Ruopp et al., *Children at the Center*.

5. Edgar Klugman and Lana Hostetler, "Early Childhood Job Titles: One Step Toward Professional Status," *Young Children* 37 (September 1982):15.

6. Ronald Reagan, 17 October 1981, cited in June Sale, "An Open Letter to President Reagan on Child Care Staff," *Young Children* 37 (March 1982):63.

7. Reagan, 3 October 1981, cited in ibid.

8. Edward Zigler and Jody Goodman, "The Battle for Day Care in America: A View from the Trenches," in Zigler and Gordon, eds., *Day Care*, p. 340.

9. Alison Clarke-Stewart, *Child Care in the Family*, p. 101.

10. Sheila Kamerman, *Parenting in an Unresponsive Society*, p. 51; p. 126.

11. *Wall Street Journal*, 20 April 1981.

12. See Klugman and Hostetler, "Early Childhood Job Titles"; William Ade, "Professionalization and Its Implications for the Field of Early Childhood Education," *Young Children* 37 (March 1982); Millie Almy "Day Care and Early Childhood Education," in Zigler and Gordon, eds., *Day Care*.

13. Barbara Beatty, "Historical Factors Affecting the Status and Pay of Preschool Teaching," draft paper, 1982.

14. Glenn Doman, *How to Teach Your Baby to Read* (New York: Dolphin Books, 1975); Doman, *Teach Your Baby Math* (New York: Simon and Schuster, 1979); Joan Beck, *How to Raise a Brighter Child* (New York: Pocket Books, 1975).

15. Margaret Steinfels, *Who's Minding the Children?*, p. 106.

16. Jerome Kagan, *Understanding Children*, p. 36.

17. Sally Provence, Audrey Naylor, and June Patterson, *The Challenge of Day Care*, pp. 120-121.

18. Ruopp et al., *Children at the Center*, pp. 140-149.

19. Martha Mattingly, "Sources of Stress and Burnout in Professional Child Care Work," *Child Care Quarterly* (Summer 1977):131-132.

20. Whitebook et al., "Who's Minding the Child Care Workers?"

21. Susan Aronson and Peggy Pizzo, "Health and Safety Issues in Day Care," *Policy Issues in Day Care: Summaries of 21 Papers* (Washington, D.C.: U.S. Department of Health, Education, and Welfare), p. 111.

22. Herbert Freudenberger, "Burn-Out: Occupational Hazard of the Child Care Worker," *Child Care Quarterly* (Summer 1977):90-91.

23. Christina Maslach and Ayala Pines, "The Burn-Out Syndrome in the Day Care Setting," *Child Care Quarterly* (Summer 1977):101, 102.

24. Ibid., p. 108.

25. Ibid., p. 129.

26. Ibid., p. 105.

27. Jean Baker Miller, *Toward a New Psychology of Women*, p. 6.

28. Ibid., p. 8.

29. Ibid., p. 10.

30. Ibid., p. 11.

31. Ruopp et al., *Children at the Center*, p. 161.

Chapter 6

1. Judith Rubenstein, Carollee Howes, and Patricia Boyle, "A Two-Year Follow-up of Infants in Community-Based Day Care," *Journal of Child Psychology and Psychiatry* 22 (1981):210.
2. Suzanne Woolsey, "Pied Piper Politics and the Child-Care Debate," p. 134.
3. Ibid.
4. Sheila B. Kamerman, *Parenting in an Unresponsive Society*, p. 53.
5. Woolsey, "Pied Piper Politics," p. 132.
6. U.S. Department of Health, Education, and Welfare, *Families Today, A Research Sampler on Families and Children*, p. 310.
7. Ibid., p. 300.
8. General Mills American Family Report, *Families at Work*, p. 33.
9. James Walters and Lynda Walters, "Parent-Child Relationships: A Review, 1970-1979," *Journal of Marriage and the Family* 42 (November 1980):81.
10. *Boston Globe*, 8 July 1982, p. 40.
11. U.S. Department of Health, Education, and Welfare, *Families Today*, p. 388.
12. Ibid., p. 398.
13. General Mills, *Families at Work*, p. 28.
14. Walters and Walters, "Parent-Child Relationships," p. 92.
15. U.S. Department of Health, Education, and Welfare, *Families Today*, p. 400.
16. Pamela Daniels and Kathy Weingarten, *Sooner or Later*, p. 131.
17. Ibid., p. 127.
18. Ibid., p. 128.
19. U.S. Department of Health, Education, and Welfare, *Families Today*, p. 315.
20. Phyllis Moen, "The Two-Provider Family: Problems and Potentials," in Michael Lamb, ed., *Nontraditional Families*, p. 37.
21. *Radcliffe College Quarterly* (June 1979):12, 13.
22. *Radcliffe College Quarterly* (December 1982):12.
23. *American Bar Association Journal* (August 1982):906.
24. *New York Times*, 13 August 1981, pp. C1, C9.
25. Anita Shreve, "Careers and the Lure of Motherhood," *New York Times Magazine*, 21 November 1982, pp. 40-41, 48.
26. *Boston Globe*, 21 November 1982, p. A22.

Chapter 7

1. Marcy Whitebook et al., "Who's Minding the Child Care Workers?," note 10.

2. Robert Halpern, "Surviving the Competition," *Young Children* 37 (July 1982):27.

3. *Miami Herald*, 22 September 1982.

4. Whitebook et al., "Who's Minding the Child Care Workers?," p. 4.

5. Christine McPartland, "Who's Minding the Children?," *Boston Magazine* (October 1982):142-143.

6. *Parents Magazine* (September 1982):76.

7. *Boston Globe Magazine*, 24 October 1982, p. 50.

8. McPartland, "Who's Minding the Children?," p. 200.

9. W. Gary Winget, "The Dilemma of Affordable Child Care," in Zigler and Gordon, eds., *Day Care*, p. 354.

10. Pamela Reeves, "Sorry, We Don't Accept Babies," *Working Mother* (July 1982):63, 91.

11. U.S. Department of the Treasury, Internal Revenue Service, *Child and Disabled Dependent Care*, publication 503.

12. *Boston Globe*, 16 July 1982, p. 19.

13. Ibid., 13 October 1982, p. 45.

14. Progress Report 1978-1981, Hebrew Rehabilitation Center for the Aged, Roslindale, Mass., unpaged.

Chapter 8

1. Sally Provence, Audrey Naylor, and June Patterson, *The Challenge of Daycare*, p. 81.

2. Alison Clarke-Stewart, *Day Care*, pp. 66-67.

3. Margaret Steinfels, *Who's Minding the Children?*, p. 110.

4. Provence, Naylor, and Patterson, *Challenge of Daycare*, p. 210.

5. Beatrice Glickman and Nesha Springer, *Who Cares for the Baby?*, pp. 210, 213.

6. Carol Seefeldt, *A Curriculum for Child Care Centers*, pp. 256-257.

7. U.S. Department of Health, Education, and Welfare, *The Appropriateness of the Federal Interagency Day Care Requirements*, p. 64.

8. Jerome Kagan, Richard Kearsley, and Philip Zelazo, *Infancy: Its Place in Human Development*, pp. 186-187.

9. Ibid., p. 267.

10. Polly Greenberg, *Day Care Do-It-Yourself Staff Growth Program*, pp. 293-294.

11. Julius Richmond and Juel Janis, "Health Care Services for Children in Day Care Programs," in Zigler and Gordon, eds., *Day Care*, p. 447.

12. Ibid., p. 449.

13. Susan Aronson and Peggy Pizzo, "Health and Safety Issues in Day Care," *Policy Issues in Day Care: Summaries of 21 Papers* (Washington, D.C.: U.S. Department of Health, Education, and Welfare), p. 112.

14. S.H. Gehlbach et al., "Spread of Disease by Fecal-Oral Route in Day Nurseries," *Health Service Report* 88 (April 1973):320-322.

15. *Washington Post*, 26 November 1982, p. A12.

16. Stanley H. Schuman, "Day-Care-Associated Infection: More than Meets the Eye," *Journal of the American Medical Association* 249 (7 January 1983):76.

17. J.B. Weissman et al, "The Role of Preschool Children and Day Care Centers in the Spread of Shigellosis in Urban Communities," *Journal of Pediatrics* 84 (June 1974):797-802.

18. Weissman et al., "Shigellosis in Day-Care Centres," *Lancet* (11 January 1975):88-90.

19. M.L. Rosenberg et al., "Shigellosis in the United States: Ten-Year Review of Nationwide Surveillance, 1964-1973," *American Journal of Epidemiology* 104 (November 1976):543-551.

20. R.E. Black et al., "Giardiasis in Day-Care Centers: Evidence of Person-to-Person Transmission," *Pediatrics* 60 (October 1977):486-491.

21. G. Storch et al., "Viral Hepatitis Associated with Day-Care Centers," *Journal of the American Medical Association* 242 (5 October 1979):1514-1518; p. 1514.

22. S.C. Hadler et al., "Hepatitis A in Day-Care Centers," *New England Journal of Medicine* 302 (29 May 1980):1222-1227; p. 1222.

23. Hadler et al., "Risk Factors for Hepatitis A in Day-Care Centers," *Journal of Infectious Diseases* 145 (February 1982):255-261; p. 255.

24. A.A. Vernon, C. Schnable, and D. Francis, "A Large Outbreak of Hepatitis A in a Day-Care Center: Association with Non-Toilet-Trained Children and Persistence of IGM Antibody to Hepatitis A Virus," *American Journal of Epidemiology* 115 (March 1982):325-331.

25. M.W. Benenson et al., "A Military Community Outbreak of Hepatitis Type A Related to Transmission in a Child Care Facility," *American Journal of Epidemiology* 112 (October 1980):471-481.

26. R.J. Silva, "Hepatitis and the Need for Adequate Standards in Federally Supported Day Care," *Child Welfare* 59 (July-August 1980): 387-400.

27. J.T. Ward et al., "Hemophilus Influenzae Type B Disease in a Day-Care Center. Report of an Outbreak," *Journal of Pediatrics* 92 (May 1978): 713-717.

28. C.M. Ginsberg et al., "Haemophilus Influenzae Type B Disease. Incidence in a Day-Care Center," *Journal of the American Medical Association* 238 (15 August 1977):604-607; p. 604.

29. R.F. Pass et al., "Cytomegalovirus Infection in a Day-Care Center," *New England Journal of Medicine* 307 (19 August 1982):477-479.

Chapter 9

1. Betty Friedan, *The Second Stage*, p. 75.
2. Erik Erikson, *Childhood and Society*, pp. 247-251.
3. Edward Zigler and Jody Goodman, "The Battle for Day Care in America: A View from the Trenches," in Zigler and Gordon, eds., *Day Care*, p. 348.
4. National Association for the Education of Young Children, 1982 Annual Conference, Preliminary Program, p. 19.
5. Tucson Association for Child Care, Inc., "Sick Child Home Health Care Program," flyer, May, 1982.

Chapter 10

1. See table A-2.
2. Richard Ruopp et al., *Children at the Center*.
3. Jay Belsky and Laurence Steinberg, "The Effects of Day Care: A Critical Review."
4. Jay Belsky, Laurence Steinberg, and Ann Walker, "The Ecology of Day Care," in Lamb, ed., *Nontraditional Families*, pp. 71-116.
5. Michael Rutter, "Social-Emotional Consequences of Day Care for Preschool Children."
6. See table A-2.
7. M. Ainsworth and B. Wittig, "Attachment and Exploratory Behavior of One-Year-Olds in a Strange Situation," in Foss, ed., *Determinants of Infant Behavior* (London: Methuen, 1969).
8. See table A-2.
9. Belsky, Steinberg, and Walker, "Ecology of Day Care," p. 90.
10. Ibid., p. 94.
11. Belsky and Steinberg, "Effects of Day Care," p. 931.
12. Rutter, "Social-Emotional Consequences," p. 20.
13. M. Cochran, "A Comparison of Group Day and Family Child-Rearing Patterns in Sweden," *Child Development* 48 (1977):702-707.
14. Jerome Kagan, Richard Kearsley, and Philip Zelazo, *Infancy: Its Place in Human Development*.
15. Ibid., p. 260.
16. Ibid., pp. 260-262.
17. Rutter, "Social-Emotional Consequences," p. 21.
18. Ruopp et al., *Children at the Center*, p. 9.
19. John R. Nelson, Jr., "The Politics of Federal Day Care Regulation," in Zigler and Gordon, eds., *Day Care*, p. 298.

20. Ruopp et al., *Children at the Center*, p. 11.

21. Marcy Whitebook et al., "Who's Minding the Child Care Workers?"

22. Karen VanderVen, Martha Mattingly, and Marian Morris, "Principles and Guidelines for Child Care Personnel Preparation Programs."

23. David Elkind, "Child Development and Early Childhood Education: Where Do We Stand Today?," *Young Children* 36 (July 1981):3.

24. Alison Clarke-Stewart, *Child Care in the Family*, p. XIV.

Chapter 11

1. General Mills, *Families at Work*, p. 31.
2. Alison Clarke-Stewart, *Day Care*, p. 21.
3. Valerie Suransky, *The Erosion of Childhood*, p. 185.
4. Selma Fraiberg, *Every Child's Birthright: In Defense of Mothering*, p. 87.
5. Ibid., p. 80.
6. Ibid., pp. 81-82.
7. Ibid., p. 86.
8. *Library Journal* 102 (1 October 1977):2070.
9. Sally Provence, Audrey Naylor, and June Patterson, *The Challenge of Daycare*, p. 223.
10. Ibid., p. 225.
11. Ibid., p. 227.
12. Ibid., p. 231.
13. Ibid., p. 232.
14. Ibid., p. 234.
15. David Elkind, *The Hurried Child*, p. 135.
16. Ibid., pp. 101-102.
17. Ibid., pp. 102-103.
18. Burton White, "Should You Stay Home With Your Baby?," *Young Children* 36 (November 1981):14.
19. Donald J. Cohen, *Serving Preschool Children*, p. 3.
20. National Association for the Education of Young Children, 1982 Annual Conference, Preliminary Program, p. 4.
21. Suzanne Woolsey, "Pied Piper Politics and the Child-Care Debate," p. 143.

Chapter 12

1. Suzanne Woolsey, "Pied Piper Politics and the Child-Care Debate," p. 127.

2. U.S. Bureau of the Census, *Trends in Child Care Arrangements of Working Mothers*, p. 3.

3. Woolsey, "Piped Piper Politics," p. 134; *Wall Street Journal* 26 October 1982; *Legal Times* 16 August 1982.

4. Mary D. Keyserling, *Windows on Day Care*; Sheila B. Kamerman, *Parenting in an Unresponsive Society*; Margaret Steinfels, *Who's Minding the Children?*

5. Joseph H. Stevens, Jr., Research Review, "The National Day Care Home Study: Family Day Care in the United States," *Young Children* 37 (May 1982):59-66.

6. Ibid., p. 60.

7. Ibid., p. 64.

8. Much of the historical information is drawn from Steinfels, *Who's Minding the Children?* and Samuel Braun and Esther Edwards, *History and Theory of Early Childhood Education.*

9. Braun and Edwards, *History and Theory*, p. 61.

10. Ibid.

11. Steinfels, *Who's Minding the Children?*

12. Arnold Gesell and Frances Ilg, *Infant and Child in the Culture of Today*, p. IX.

13. C. Bereiter and S. Engleman, *Teaching Disadvantaged Children in the Preschool* (Englewood Cliffs, N.J.: Prentice Hall, 1966); Benjamin Bloom, *Stability and Change in Human Characteristics* (New York: John Wiley and Sons, 1964); James McV. Hunt, *Intelligence and Experience* (New York: Ronald Press, 1961).

14. Woolsey, "Pied Piper Politics," p. 130.

15. U.S. Department of Labor, *Child Care Centers Sponsored by Employers and Labor Unions in the United States* (Washington, D.C.: Office of the Secretary, Women's Bureau, 1980), p. 2.

16. Among the most frequently mentioned successes are day-care centers sponsored by the Stride Rite Corporation, Boston, Mass., Hoffman-LaRoche, Inc., Nutley, New Jersey; and Intermedics, Inc., Freeport, Tex.

17. U.S. Department of Labor, *Child Care Centers*, p. 2.

18. Woolsey, "Pied Piper Politics," p. 135.

19. U.S. Department of Labor, *Child Care Centers*, p. 7.

20. S. Fosburg, *Family Day-Care in the U.S.*: Summary of Findings (Washington, D.C.: U.S. Department of Health and Human Services, 1981).

21. Gesell and Ilg, *Infant and Child*, p. 259.

Chapter 13

1. James A. Levine, "The Prospects and Dilemmas of Child Care Information and Referral," in Zigler and Gordon, eds., *Day Care.*

2. *New York Times*, 14 June 1982, p. A16; John Tydeman et al., *Teletext and Videotex in the United States* (Menlo Park, Cal.: Institute for the Future, 1982).

3. *New York Times*, 3 June 1982, p. 8.

4. Alice Rossi, "A Biosocial Perspective on Parenting," p. 25.

5. Eunice Corfman, "Married Men: Work and Family," summarizing the work of Joseph Pleck, in Corfman, ed., *Families Today: A Research Sampler on Families and Children*, I, p. 409.

6. Editorial Research Reports, "Work Life in the 1980s," *Congressional Quarterly* (1981):55.

7. Ibid.; General Mills, *Families at Work*, p. 47.

8. General Mills, *Families at Work*, p. 47.

9. Catalyst, *Corporations and Two Career Families*, p. 45.

10. General Mills, *Families at Work*, p. 47.

11. Ibid., p. 56.

12. *New York Times*, 27 January 1981, p. D5.

13. Ibid.

14. *New York Times*, 7 December 1981, p. B18.

15. *New York Times*, 12 December 1982, p. 57.

16. Michael Lamb et al., "Varying Degrees of Paternal Involvement in Infant Care: Attitudinal and Behavioral Correlates," in Lamb, ed., *Nontraditional Families*, p. 118.

17. Alison Clarke-Stewart, *Child Care in the Family*, p. 97; p. 103; Amitai Etzioni, *An Immodest Agenda: Rebuilding America before the Twenty-First Century* (New York: McGraw-Hill Book Company, 1983), pp. 115-116.

18. Pamela Daniels and Kathy Weingarten, *Sooner or Later*, pp. 3-4.

19. Ibid., p. 5.

20. Graeme Russell, "Shared-Caregiving Families: An Australian Study," in Lamb, ed., *Nontraditional Families*, p. 169.

21. Rossi, "A Biosocial Perspective," p. 16.

22. Hans Christian Andersen, *The Emperor's New Clothes* (Odense, Denmark: Skandinavisk Bogforlag, 1979).

Chapter 14

1. Amitai Etzioni, *An Immodest Agenda: Rebuilding America before the Twenty-First Century* (New York: McGraw-Hill Book Company, 1983), p. 116.

2. Kenneth Keniston, *All Our Children*, p. 99.

3. Erik Erikson, *Childhood and Society*, p. 267.

4. Robert A. Dutch, *Roget's Thesaurus* (New York: St. Martin's Press, 1965), p. 426.

Bibliography

Achenbach, Thomas M. *Research in Developmental Psychology: Concepts, Strategies, Methods*. New York: Free Press, 1978.

American Academy of Political and Social Science. "Young Children and Social Policy." *Annals* 461 (May 1982).

Belsky, Jay, and Steinberg, Laurence. "The Effects of Day Care: A Critical Review." *Child Development* 49 (1978):929-949.

Berardo, Felix M., ed. "Decade Review: Family Research 1970-1979." *Journal of Marriage and the Family* 42 (November 1980).

Bettelheim, Bruno. *The Children of the Dream*. New York: Macmillan Co., 1969.

Boston Women's Health Book Collective. *Ourselves and Our Children*. New York: Random House, 1978.

Braun, Samuel J., and Edwards, Esther P. *History and Theory of Early Childhood Education*. Worthington, Ohio: Charles A. Jones Publishing Co., 1972.

Brewer, Gail S. *What Every Pregnant Woman Should Know*. New York: Random House, 1977.

Bronfenbrenner, Urie. *Two Worlds of Childhood: U.S. and U.S.S.R.* New York: Pocket Books, 1973.

Bruner, Jerome, and Garton, Alison, eds. *Human Growth and Development*. Oxford: Oxford University Press, 1978.

Catalyst. *Corporations and Two-Career Families: Directions for the Future*. New York: Catalyst Career and Family Center, n.d.

Clarke-Stewart, Alison. *Child Care in the Family*. New York: Academic Press, 1977.

______ . *Daycare*. Cambridge, Mass.: Harvard University Press, 1982.

Cohen, Donald J. *Serving Preschool Children*, vol. 3. Washington, D.C.: U.S. Government Printing Office, 1974.

Corfman, Eunice, ed. *Families Today: A Research Sampler on Families and Children*, vol. 1. Rockville, Md.: U.S. Department of Health, Education, and Welfare, n.d.

Daniels, Pamela, and Weingarten, Kathy. *Sooner or Later*. New York: W. W. Norton and Co., 1982.

Elkind, David. *The Hurried Child*. Reading, Mass.: Addison-Wesley Publishing Co., 1981.

Elkind, David, and Weiner, Irving B. *Child Development: A Core Approach*. New York: John Wiley and Sons, 1972.

Erikson, Erik H. *Childhood and Society*. New York: W.W. Norton and Co., 1950.

Fein, Greta G., and Clarke-Stewart, Alison. *Day Care in Context*. New York: John Wiley and Sons, 1973.

Fraiberg, Selma. *The Magic Years*. New York: Charles Scribner's Sons, 1959.

______ . *Every Child's Birthright: In Defense of Mothering*. New York: Basic Books, Inc., 1977.

Friedan, Betty. *The Second Stage*. New York: Summit Books, 1981.

Gardner, Howard. *Developmental Psychology*. Boston: Little, Brown and Co., 1982.

General Mills American Family Report. *Families at Work*. Minneapolis: General Mills, 1981.

Gesell, Arnold, and Ilg, Frances L. *Infant and Child in the Culture of Today*. New York: Harper and Brothers Publishers, 1943.

Glickman, Beatrice M., and Springer, Nesha B. *Who Cares for the Baby?* New York: Schocken Books, 1978.

Greenberg, Polly. *Day Care Do-It-Yourself Staff Growth Program*. Washington, D.C.: The Growth Program, 1975.

Joffe, Carole E. *Friendly Intruders: Childcare Professionals and Family Life*. Berkeley: University of California Press, 1977.

Kagan, Jerome. *Understanding Children*. New York: Harcourt, Brace, Jovanovich, 1971.

Kagan, Jerome; Kearsley, Richard B.; and Zelazo, Philip R. *Infancy: Its Place in Human Development*. Cambridge, Mass.: Harvard University Press, 1978.

Kamerman, Sheila B. *Parenting in an Unresponsive Society*. New York: Free Press, 1980.

Kappelman, M.M., and Ackerman, P.R. *Parents After Thirty*. New York: Rawson, Wade Publishers, Inc., 1980.

Keniston, Kenneth, and The Carnegie Council on Children. *All Our Children*. New York: Harcourt, Brace, Jovanovich, 1977.

Keyserling, Mary Dublin. *Windows on Day Care*. New York: National Council of Jewish Women, 1972.

Klaus, Marshall H.; Leger, Treville; and Trause, Mary Anne, eds. *Maternal Attachment and Mothering Disorders: A Round Table*. Sausalito, Calif.: Johnson and Johnson Baby Products Co., 1974.

Lamb, Michael E., ed. *Nontraditional Families: Parenting and Child Development*. Hillsdale, N.J.: Lawrence Erlbaum Associates, 1982.

Light, Richard J., and Pillemer, David B. "Numbers and Narrative: Combining Their Strengths in Research Reviews." *Harvard Educational Review* 52 (1982):1-26.

McBride, Angela Barron. *The Growth and Development of Mothers*. New York: Harper and Row, 1973.

McCauley, Carole S. *Pregnancy After 35*. New York: E.P. Dutton and Co., Inc., 1976.

Miller, Jean Baker. *Toward a New Psychology of Women*. Boston: Beacon Press, 1976.

Mills, Belen Collantes, ed. *Understanding the Young Child and His Curriculum*. New York: Macmillan Co., 1972.

Papalia, Diane E., and Olds, Sally Wendkos. *A Child's World*. New York: McGraw-Hill Book Co., 1975.

Piaget, Jean. *The Construction of Reality in the Child*. New York: Basic Books, 1954.

Pillemer, David B., and Light, Richard J. "Synthesizing Outcomes: How to Use Research Evidence from Many Studies." *Harvard Educational Review* 50 (1980):176-195.

Pleck, Joseph H. "The Work-Family Role System." *Social Problems* 24 (1977):417-427.

Price, Jane. *You're Not Too Old to Have a Baby*. New York: Farrar, Straus, Giroux, 1977.

Provence, Sally; Naylor, Audrey; and Patterson, June. *The Challenge of Daycare*. New Haven: Yale University Press, 1977.

Roby, Pamela, ed. *Child Care—Who Cares?* New York: Basic Books, 1973.

Rossi, Alice S. "A Biosocial Perspective on Parenting." *Daedalus* (Spring 1977):1-31.

Ruopp, Richard; Travers, Jeffrey; Glantz, Frederic; and Coelen, Craig. *Children at the Center*. Cambridge, Mass.: Abt Associates, 1979.

Rutter, Michael. "Social-Emotional Consequences of Day Care for Preschool Children." *American Journal of Orthopsychiatry* 51 (January 1981):4-28.

Schaffer, Rudolph. *Mothering*. Cambridge, Mass.: Harvard University Press, 1977.

Seefeldt, Carol. *A Curriculum for Child Care Centers*. Columbus, Ohio: Charles E. Merrill Co., 1974.

Sidel, Ruth. *Women and Child Care in China*. Baltimore: Penguin Books, 1973.

Steiner, Gilbert Y. *The Children's Cause*. Washington, D.C.: Brookings Institute, 1976.

Steinfels, Margaret O'Brien. *Who's Minding the Children?* New York: Simon and Schuster, 1973.

Suransky, Valerie P. *The Erosion of Childhood*. Chicago: University of Chicago Press, 1982.

U.S. Bureau of the Census, Current Population Reports, series P-23, no. 117. *Trends in Child Care Arrangements of Working Mothers*. Washington, D.C.: U.S. Government Printing Office, 1982.

U.S. Commission on Civil Rights. *Child Care and Equal Opportunity for Women*. Washington, D.C.: U.S. Commission on Civil Rights, June 1981.

U.S. Department of Health and Human Services. *Amniocentesis for Prenatal Chromosomal Diagnosis*. Atlanta, 1980.

U.S. Department of Health, Education, and Welfare. *The Appropriateness of the Federal Interagency Day Care Requirements*. Washington, D.C.: Office of the Assistant Secretary for Planning and Evaluation, 1978.

______. *Families Today, a Research Sampler on Families and Children*. Rockville, Md.: NIMH Science Monographs 1, n.d.

______. *Guides for Day Care Licensing*. Washington, D.C., n.d.

U.S. Department of Labor. *Child Care Centers Sponsored by Employers and Labor Unions in the United States*. Washington, D.C.: Office of the Secretary, Women's Bureau, 1980.

______. *Employers and Child Care: Establishing Services Through the Workplace*. Washington, D.C.: Office of the Secretary, Women's Bureau, January 1981.

VanderVen, Karen; Mattingly, Martha; and Morris, Marian. "Principles and Guidelines for Child Care Personnel Preparation Programs." *Child Care Quarterly* 11 (Fall 1982).

Whitebook, Marcy; Howes, Carollee; Darrah, Rory; and Friedman, Jane. "Who's Minding the Child Care Workers?" *Children Today* (January-February 1981), 2.

Woolsey, Suzanne H. "Pied Piper Politics and the Child-Care Debate." *Daedalus* (Spring, 1977):127-145.

Zigler, Edward F., and Gordon, Edmund W., eds. *Day Care: Scientific and Social Policy Issues*. Boston: Auburn House Publishing Co., 1982.

Zigler, Edward, and Muenchow, Susan. "Infant Day Care and Infant-Care Leaves." *American Psychologist* 38 (1983):91-94.

Index

About the Author

Marian Blum is the educational director of the Wellesley College Child Study Center. The center, a laboratory nursery school for the Psychology Department of Wellesley College, offers part-time programs for children aged two to five. Mrs. Blum previously has directed other part-time as well as full-time facilities for preschoolers. She has had extensive professional experience working with young children, their teachers, and their parents. In addition, she has taught college and university courses in child development and early-childhood education and has supervised student teachers in approximately one-hundred nursery schools, day-care centers, and kindergartens in Greater Boston. Mrs. Blum is a graduate of Smith College and the Graduate School of Education, Harvard University.